CW01368420

Brutal East

Volume II

By Zupagrafika

David Navarro & Martyna Sobecka

-

Foreword: Alexander Ostrogorsky

ZUPA GRA FiKA

Contents

–

Foreword	5
Moscow. 'The House on Chicken Legs'	8
Tbilisi. 'Sky-Bridge' Housing Estate	12
Kyiv. Hotel Salute	16
Skopje. Studentski Dom 'Goce Delčev'	20
Berlin. Haus der Statistik	24
Budapest. Havanna Housing Estate	28
Minsk. 'Kukuruza' Housing Complex	32
Dombay. Hotel Amanauz	36
Buzludzha. The Monument House of the BCP	40
Press-out models	47
Author	71
Acknowledgements	72

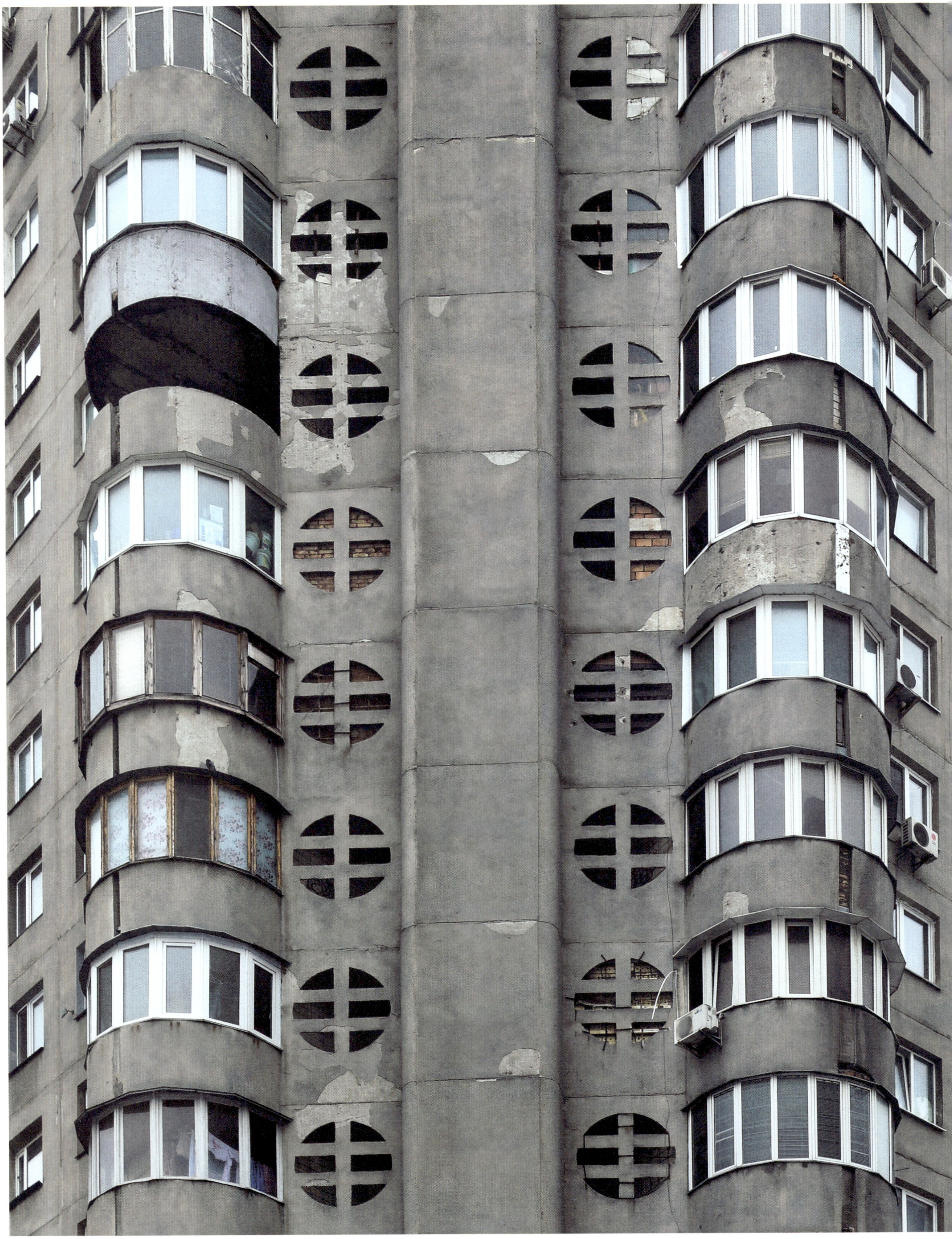

Of all the monuments of the socialist era, the *Worker and Kolkhoz Woman* by sculptor Vera Mukhina and architect Boris Iofan is seemingly one of the most recognizable in the world. A man and a woman stand on a high pedestal, thrusting forward a hammer and sickle, so that they must turn back with the other halves of their bodies for counterbalance and rest their feet firmly on the marble.

They first took this pose in Paris, at the International Exhibition in 1937. At the time there was another monumental pavilion, standing on the opposite side. It was as stable as a Doric column or a plinth, crowned with an eagle, and belonged to the Third Reich. This confrontation of the two symbols, a dynamic couple grasping tools in their hands and a gloomy eagle, was the writing on the wall, the prophecy of an impending deadly war.

After the exposition, the monument took its place at the VDNKh exhibition. At this showcase of the Soviet state, the display demonstrated the country's advancements, hiding the terrible truth about the price paid for them.

Thirty years passed. On the opposite side of the man and woman striving for communism, on Prospekt Mira, a new obstacle suddenly arose. This time it was not a hostile animal. On the contrary, it was the very utopian future to which they were heading. Infinitely distant before, it now suddenly materialized and advanced directly before them. The future took the form of a 25-storey experimental building with 480 apartments, designed by architects Andreev and Zaikin. A giant slab, with a ribbed, rough surface, blocked the view of the monumental pair and obstructed their movement. From builders of communism, aiming someplace ahead, they turned into a husband and wife returning home from work. The USSR entered the last major period of its history – the *Era of Stagnation*, which was marked not only by such architecture but also by the invasion into Czechoslovakia in 1968, which took place during construction on Prospekt Mira.

It was not only in the Soviet but in even the socialist states that architects of both the first and second worlds strove to approach the realization of the utopian ideas of early modernism. The welfare state viewed architecture, along with healthcare and pensions, as an instrument of distributing wealth, as well as control and management.

Residential tower blocks in
Obolonskyi District

Separate living space was part of the 'package' that the Soviet government promised to its loyal citizens, most of whom still lived packed together in shared apartments or barracks. The fulfilment of this promise could be anticipated for years by those on the waiting list. But the waiting makes a person even more loyal than if they receive what is expected. Nevertheless, in Moscow, it was necessary to satisfy the needs of its population as much as possible, since many Muscovites worked not only in plants and factories but also in government agencies and institutions, ensuring the movement of the state forward on the bureaucratic and ideological fronts. Experimental dwellings, towering over the mass of standard ones, were most often reserved for those Soviet citizens to whom the state had special obligations.

'The welfare state viewed architecture, along with healthcare and pensions, as an instrument of distributing wealth, as well as control and management'

However, it would be wrong to focus only on the building. It was part of the infrastructure, but in the late 1960s, it was not yet so ubiquitous. Connected to the electrical and water supply networks, as well as central heating, the building and apartments were providing access to modern civilization, installing a person into the network. The visible and perceptible elements of this network were just an expression of a complex social caste system. But flesh and blood need flesh and blood, as the song says.

The most compelling visual quality of a brutalist building is its ability to be open about its structure. The elements that make up the structure of a building are articulated by their materiality. We see seams, joints, load-bearing elements and infilling. When we look we sense someone else's gaze, one that belongs to the creator of this system.

The idea of a welfare state, regardless of the type of regime, presupposes concern for the well-being of citizens. The way in which infrastructure and buildings relate expresses this concern in the clearest manner. All forms of energy that the state accumulates, including citizen taxes, are distributed evenly and fairly. The house is a specially designed tool for accessing these streams.

Through the process of design, architecture became a reading and interpretation of social and economic orders. In this sense brutalism is quite different from its direct predecessors, modernist movements based on the egalitarian agendas of the 1920s–1930s. Tatlin's Tower was a grand symbolic gesture, in which he probably foresaw the clarity and directness of brutalism. But it was still a symbol rather than a system. Russian Constructivists as well as Bauhaus and Le Corbusier (of the pre-war period) were dreaming of larger schemes and universal laws, but their buildings were more often heterotopian shelters for modern culture surrounded by hostile environments. brutalism found itself in a completely new position, thrown into the post-war world dominated by mighty governmental agencies. This required an understanding of structure and articulation, the role of an element, and what connects them. This process is different from translating the timeless laws of beauty into a building through the instrument of proportion, which Palladio did. It also differs from the speculative re-reading of the type and typology by Aldo Rossi. This is closer to simultaneous translation, in which sounds of one language, passing through the mind of the interpreter, are transformed into sounds of another. The nuances and subtleties of the original message may be lost, but the uncertainty and ambiguity inherent in the speaker's lively speech will certainly remain.

The ubiquity and inclusiveness of this system directly depended on the fact that it did not have significant competitors, as with present-day Facebook or Google. In the countries of the Eastern Bloc, despite numerous differences in their governance, culture and history, the rigid system of command and control worked as efficiently as it could.

Within the system, there was a place not only for the residents but also for architects. They thus became both devoted adepts and critics of its language. It placed them in a privileged position, like many other specialists. Unlike the majority, they had a view of much larger portions of the system, although no one probably had a complete picture of it. Is it such a paradox that brutalism is the leader among the styles 'hated by the man on the street, loved by architects'?

But what, then, explains the relatively recent fascination with brutalism, as well as the socialist architectural heritage? Books, exhibitions, films and even computer games – is it nostalgia for something that most of the enthusiasts did not experience themselves? Or a protest against loose government policies and harsh corporate controls, disguised through the digital shells of pleasant colour schemes?

Be that as it may, the era of Big Governments ended long ago. The hopes of several generations were buried under the rubble of these ruins. New global crises, political leaders with progressive or conservative but equally radical-sounding agendas, raise new hopes. Projects made from low-tech materials and modular structures such as ship containers or bamboo rods, reimagining the remains of industrial buildings – this is, perhaps, the brutalism of a new era. Soon it will also disappear, like all the previous ones. So let us learn to appreciate its logic and grace.

Alexander Ostrogorsky
Writer on architecture and lecturer at Moscow Architecture School MARCH

Prospekt Mira
Moscow, Russia

Architects: Viktor Andreev, Trifon Zaikin
Built: 1968

25 storeys, 480 apartments
House series II-57

Moscow > 'The House on Chicken Legs'

Stretching for nearly 9 km in the northeastern part of the city, Prospekt Mira is one of the longest and oldest arteries in Moscow. Its complete reconstruction in the 1930s, instigated by the planned All-Union Agricultural Exhibition, resulted in the mass demolition of buildings erected along the old Meschanskaya Street and soon the new avenue became an interesting display of the Russian architectural trends and aspirations of the modern era. From the triumphal arch-like main entrance to the Exhibition complex, and cosmic superstructures, to prefab panel residential units and the monumental socialist *Worker and Kolkhoz Woman* sculpture, the avenue provides a comprehensive insight into the city's Soviet past. When walking past this steel monument by Vera Mukhina, a solid housing block standing on reinforced concrete stilts directly opposite the expo area immediately catches the eye. Its hypnotizing facade is made of infinite balconies laid out in a checkerboard pattern and creating the optical effect of kaleidoscope-like moving symmetrical patterns. The 25-storey construction made of large prefab

'The House on Chicken Legs' with the *Worker and Kolkhoz Woman* sculpture

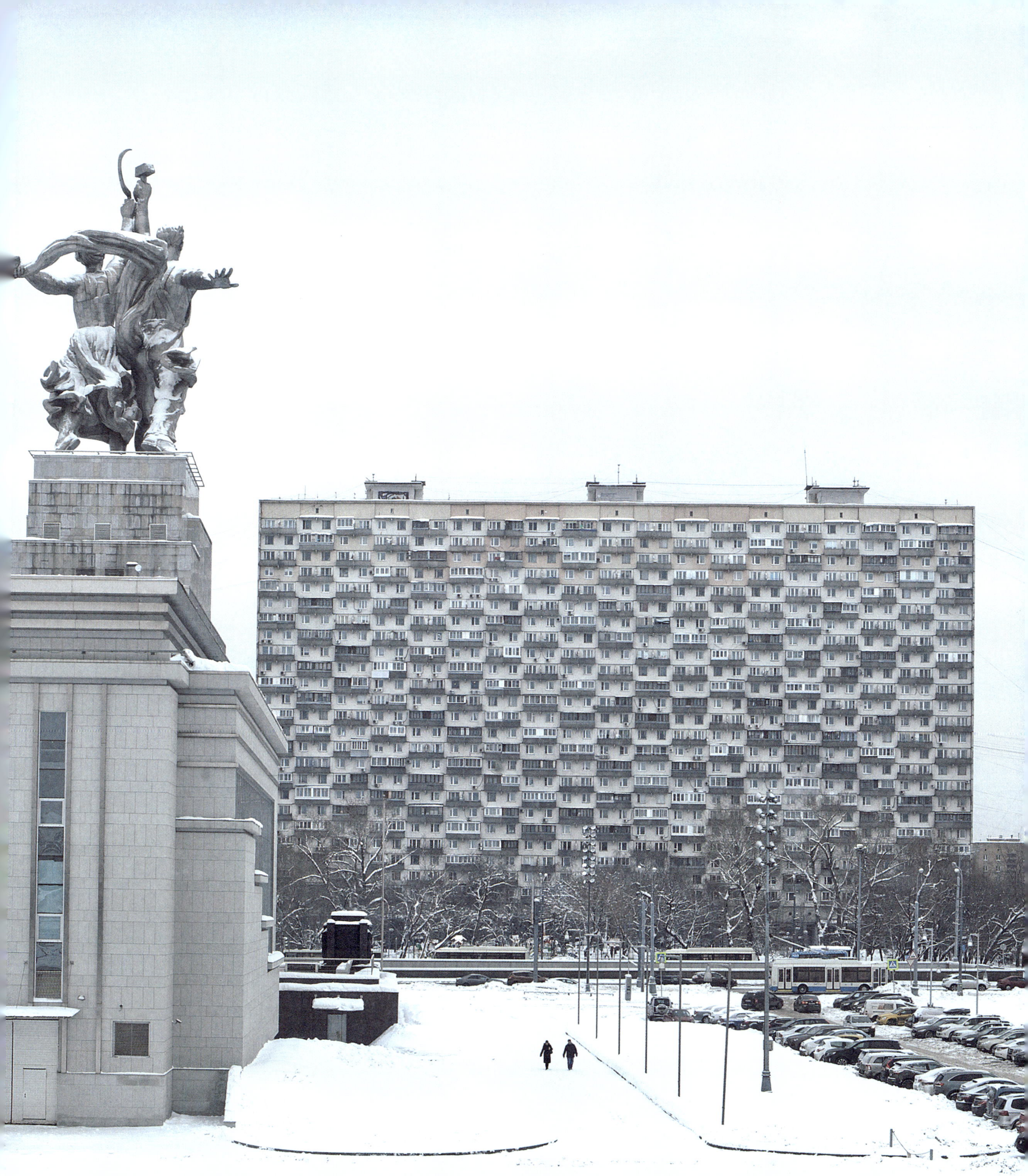

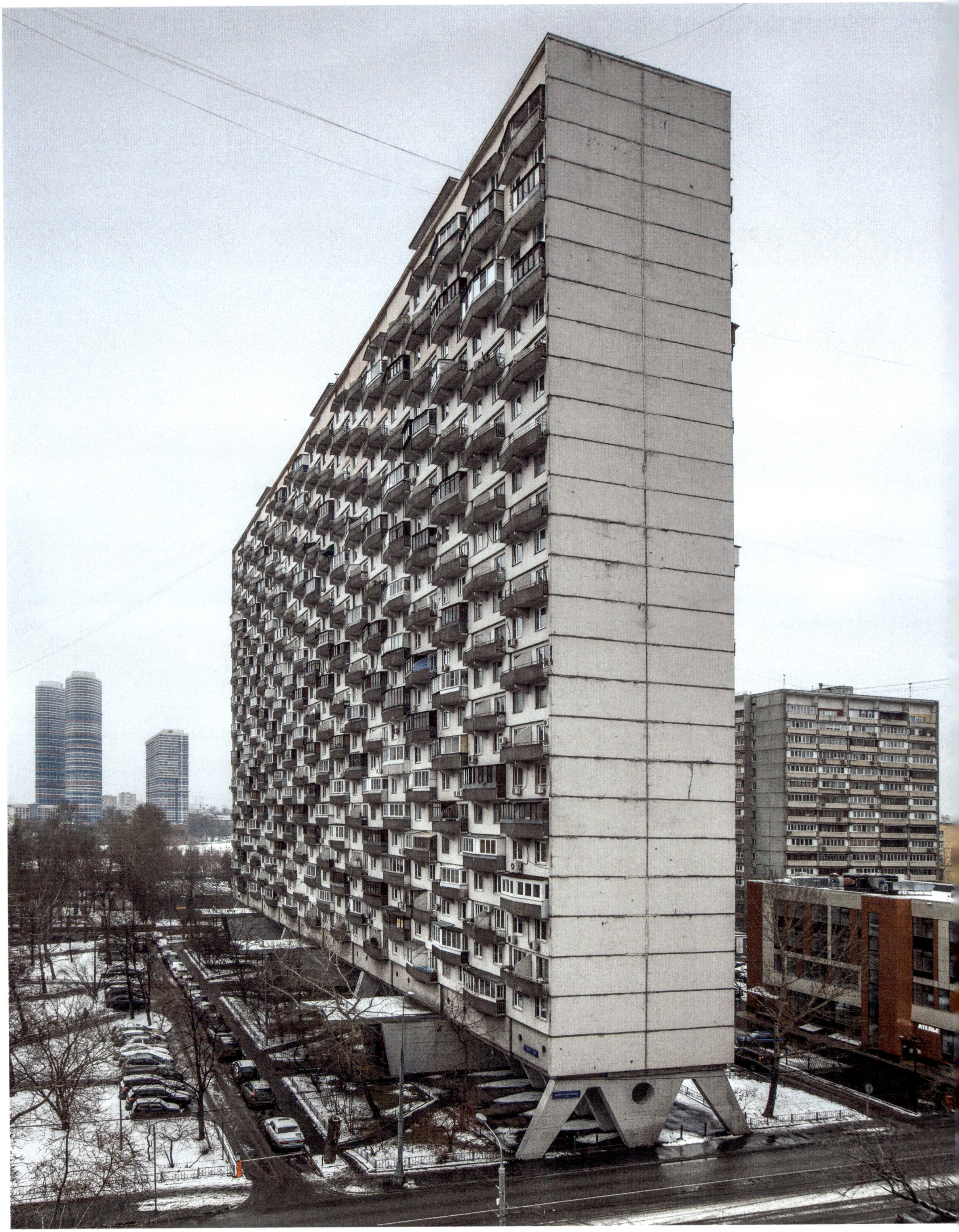
АТЕЛЬЕ

◁

Checkerboard balconies as seen from Borisa Galushkina street

△

V-shaped stilts of 'The Centipede' or 'The House of the Aviators' in Begovaya street

panels was one of the first buildings erected with this technology in Moscow by the time it was completed in 1968. The architect-engineer team Viktor Andreev and Trifon Zaikin, also known for other grand designs in Moscow, such as the neighbouring Hotel Cosmos, placed the sizeable concrete slab on 30 feather-like pillars, thus reversing the traditional construction scheme of heavy on the bottom and light on top and making the building appear to float above the surface of the ground. The method popularized by Le Corbusier and known as pilotis in the west was also put to experimental use by the Russian Constructivists who pioneered stilt supported housing in the USSR during the interwar period. As nicknamed by the Muscovites: 'The House on Chicken Legs', 'The Titanic', and 'The Centipede', built between the 1960s and 1970s, follow in the footsteps of the iconic trailblazer Narkomfin house erected in Moscow's Novinsky Boulevard in 1930.

Shalva Nutsubidze street
Tbilisi, Georgia

Architects: O. Kalandarishvili, G. Potskhishvili
Built: 1974-1976

3 residential tower blocks
connected with suspended bridges

Tbilisi > 'Sky-Bridge' Housing Estate

From Art Nouveau to Oriental, Neoclassical and finally, Soviet modern, the streets of Tbilisi take visitors on an intercontinental Euro-Asian tour. This plethora of architectural styles is also a material reminiscence of Georgia's rich but complex history. Known as the birthplace of Joseph Stalin, the country had remained under the stronger or weaker influence of Russia ever since the 19th century and when the Bolsheviks took control of the Democratic Republic of Georgia in the 1920s, Tbilisi's colourful and ornamental urban space started to visibly turn square and grey. However, it was not long before the Soviet uniformity was gradually broken by the new architectural trends originating from both Europe and Asia, and inspiring Georgian designers to pursue new approaches to construction. Following the 'cities of the future' concept explored by post-war modernists, Japanese Metabolists, and Russian Constructivists, Georgian architect Gyorgy Chakhava developed the Space City method to build one of the most spectacular brutalist structures in the country, the Ministry of Highway Construction. The idea based on erecting upwards and leaving the ground floor for natural habitat was indeed a perfect solution for the hilly terrain of Tbilisi. No wonder a similar vision was

'Sky-Bridge' tower blocks are connected with suspended pedestrian bridges

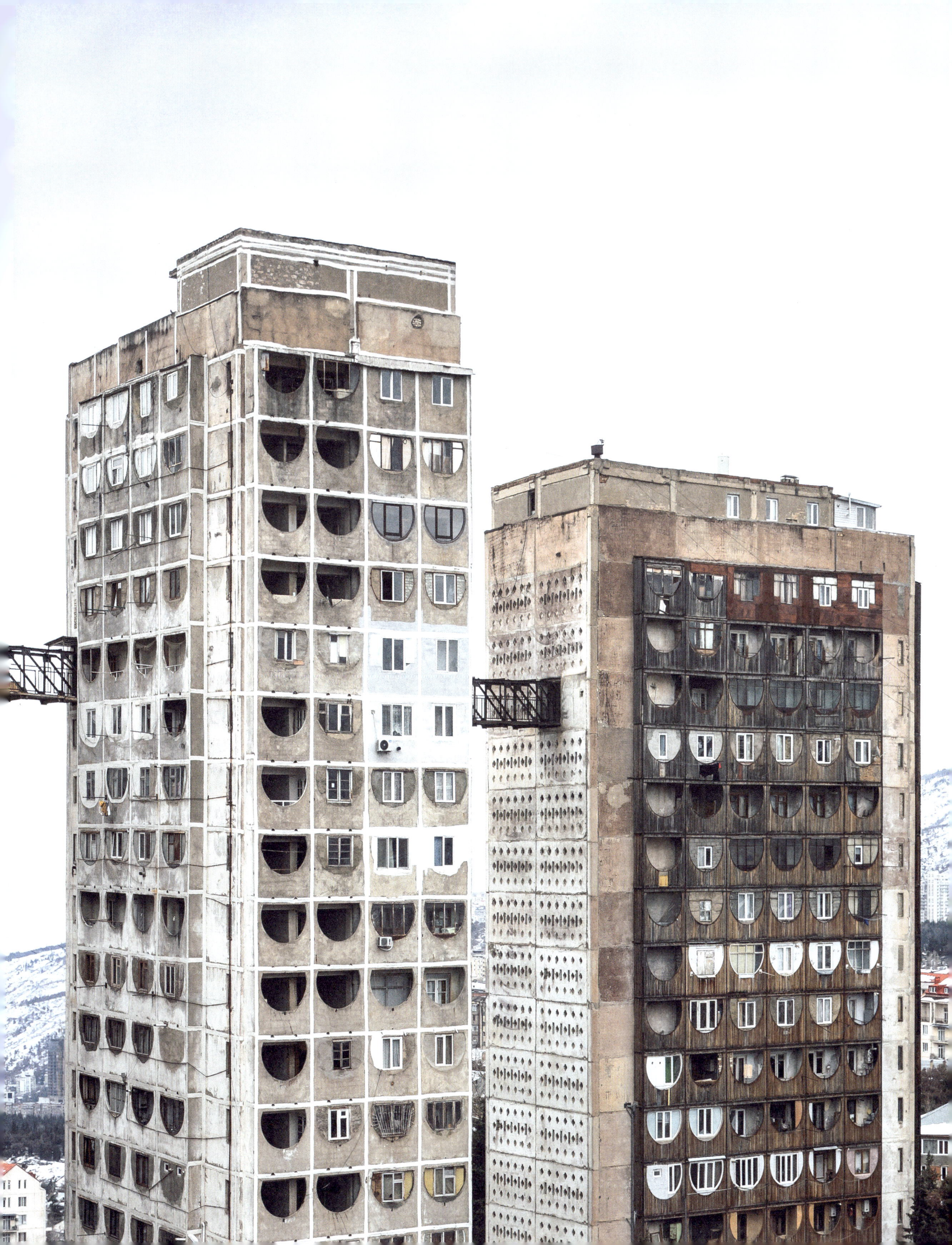

△

The bridges and lifts inside the complex are open to public use and a small fee is charged for a ride up

▷

The original facades are often modified by the inhabitants

later adopted for housing development when the duo Otar Kalandarishvili and Guizo Potskhishvili, known for their experiments with concrete, drafted a plan for residential tower blocks in the new districts of Saburtalo and Nutsubidze Plato. Three buildings, one with 16 storeys and two with nine, laid out according to the slope inclination, were erected from prefab panel blocks on a steep hill along Nutsubidze Street. The challenging topography of the site was tamed by the 'bridges in the sky', connecting the three buildings with iron passages high up at the levels of their 14th, 12th and 10th floors, respectively. The bridges do not only serve those who inhabit the blocks known as Micro I, II and III, but they are also used by the passers-by who instead of climbing up can reach the Nutsubidze plateau by taking a lift to the 14th floor of the 16-storey building and walk through the remaining two towers erected higher up. Although the lift use is not limited to the buildings' inhabitants, it might still come as a surprise that about 10 tetri (circa two euro cents) in coins must be paid for each ride up.

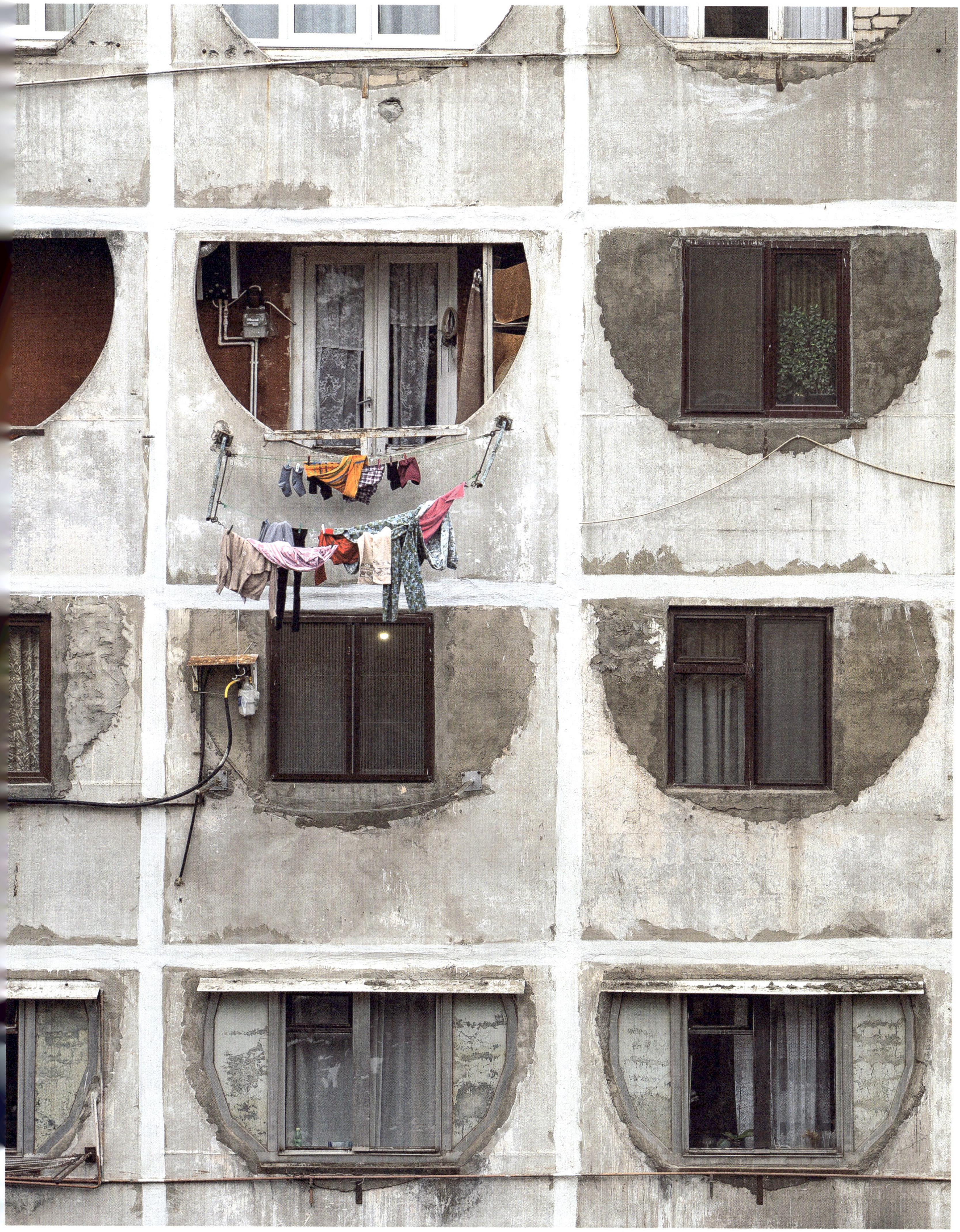

Ivana Mazepy street
Kyiv, Ukraine

Architects: A. Miletsky,
N. Slogotskaya, V. Shevchenko

Built: 1982-1984
7 storeys, 100 rooms

Kyiv > Hotel Salute

Ukraine can boast Soviet modernist architecture one will not find anywhere else in the former USSR countries, still untouched by the brutal reality of premature demolition or frivolous renovation, yet often in a poor state of disrepair and negligence due to both practical and political reasons. For many years now the structures erected under Khrushchev and Brezhnev have been as equally abundant as they were controversial in the eyes of contemporary Ukrainians. The country's stormy relation with Russia has remained an emotive issue to this day, with Ukraine trying to distance itself as much as possible from its Soviet past. The destalinization act passed in 2014 has officially detached the Ukrainian Soviet Socialist Republic's heavy load, putting its omnipresent legacy in peril at the same time. From an architectural point of view, the future of such gems as Kyiv's UFO building or Memory Park has become uncertain. Hotel Salute, proudly demonstrating its concrete curves by the Dnieper River, is one of the buildings in question that might, however, be facing less danger, at least for now. With its awe-inspiring city views, the hotel still is one of the most popular accommodations in Kyiv. Its construction began in 1982 in the central Pecherskyi district with the original cylindrical shape, the silver and

The cylindrical building was originally designed to be 12 floors high, although it only reached seven storeys

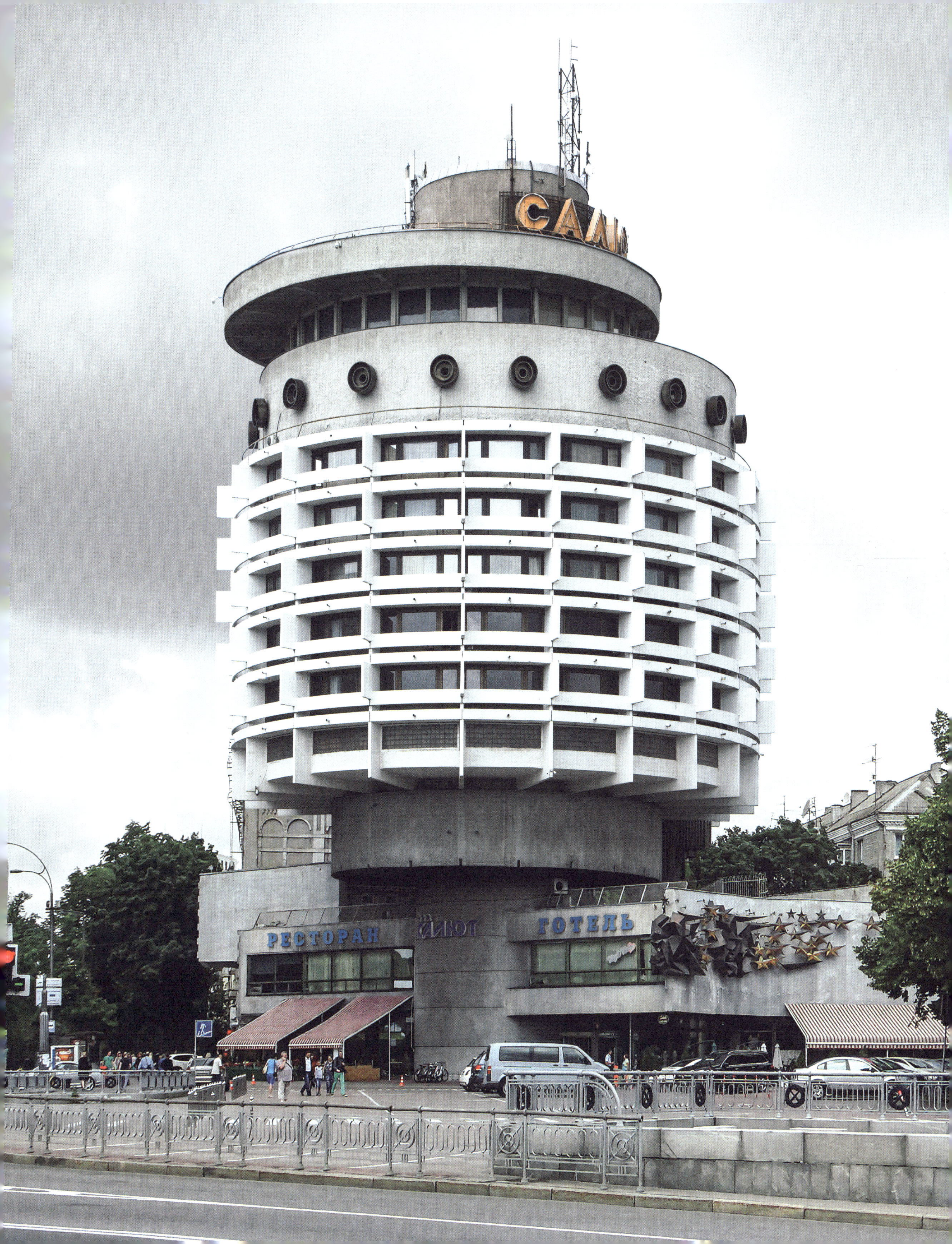
САЛЮ
РЕСТОРАН
ГОТЕЛЬ

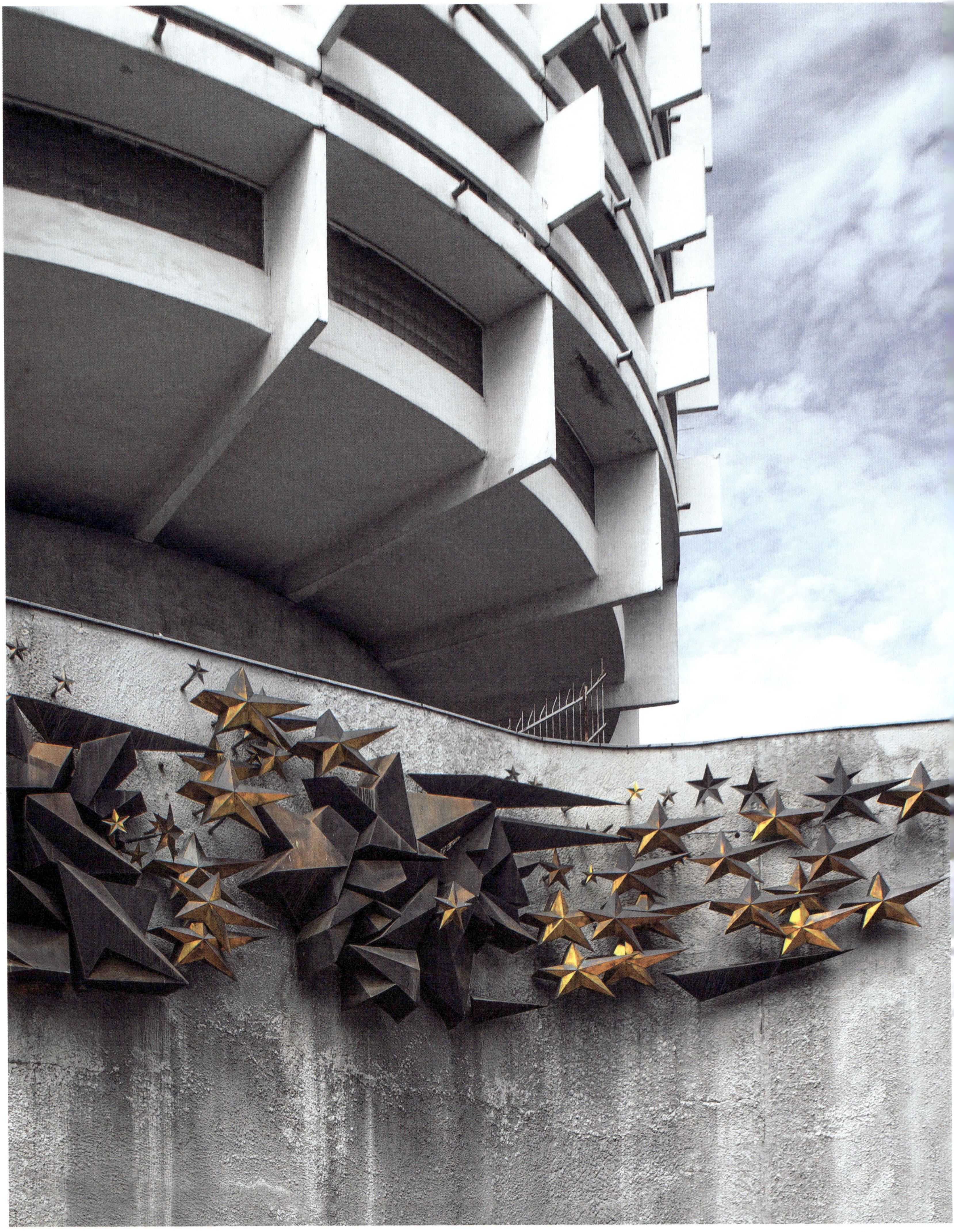

gold stars decorating its concrete base, and the hotel's very name celebrating the Salyut space stations. These were part of the USSR's first space programme carrying out scientific research between the early 1970s and 1980s.

The grandeur of those achievements was to manifest itself in the building's height – counting 12 floors, the hotel was to be one of the first skyscrapers on Kyiv's skyline. Allegedly, the architects would not yield to the communist party's attempts at making a party supervisor the building's co-author. This disobedience translated into a massive budget cut from the state and as a result, only seven stories were erected upon a foundation designed to carry a much heavier construction. The building's interior, however, is spacious enough to house a restaurant, bar and lounge located on the first floor, approximately 100 rooms on the upper floors, a lift shaft in the building's core and a spiral staircase.

Although the bold ideas behind its creation were curbed by the central power, Salute's abbreviated version embodies the might of the futuristic architectural thought of the time.

◁

The stars at the entrance symbolize fireworks (*Salyut* in Ukrainian)

△

'The Flying Saucer' State Scientific and Technical Library, aka 'UFO', built in 1971

Mitropolit Teodosij Gologanov
Skopje, North Macedonia

Architect: Georgi Konstantinovski
Built: 1969-1973

Complex of 4 tower blocks
accomodating over 1200 students

Skopje > Studentski Dom 'Goce Delčev'

The abundance of extraordinary concrete architecture pieces around every corner of Skopje, a city whose origins date back to 4000 BC., might seem striking at first glance. But when you learn its unique urban landscape was erected on the ruins left by a fatal earthquake in 1963, everything starts to make sense. Over less than half an hour, 80% of its ancient architecture was torn down, nearly 2,000 of its inhabitants lost their lives and hundreds became stranded on the streets. In the face of the tragedy, the United Nations sent in all kinds of aid, from monetary and personnel, to prefabricated panel houses to be assembled in situ. A renowned Japanese architect, Kenzō Tange, known for his affinity to post-war modernism, was also invited to shape the new urbanscape of Skopje. Together with the team of local architects, they filled the city with mighty structures made of concrete, steel and glass, such as the Central Post Office, Saint Cyril and Methodius University, State Hydrometeorological Institute, and 'Goce Delčev' student dormitory buildings. The latter is a spectacular complex of four high-rise edifices towering above the Mitropolit Teodosij Gologanov boulevard, designed by the Macedonian forerunner of brutalism, Georgi Konstantinovski. The A, B, C and D tower blocks provide single and double room abodes for over 1,200 students and are connected with

Tower Block D with balconies on side elevation, as seen from Moskovska street

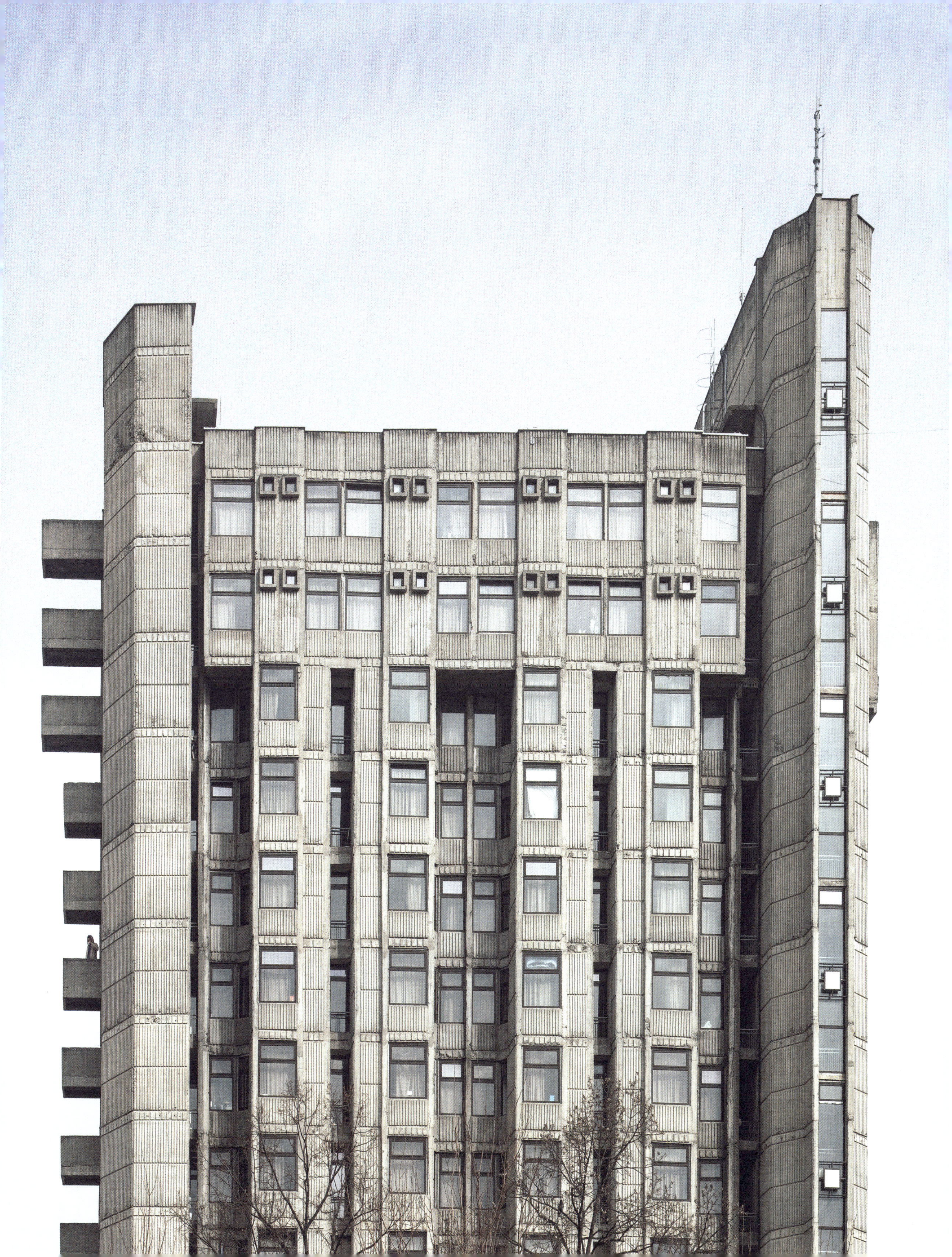

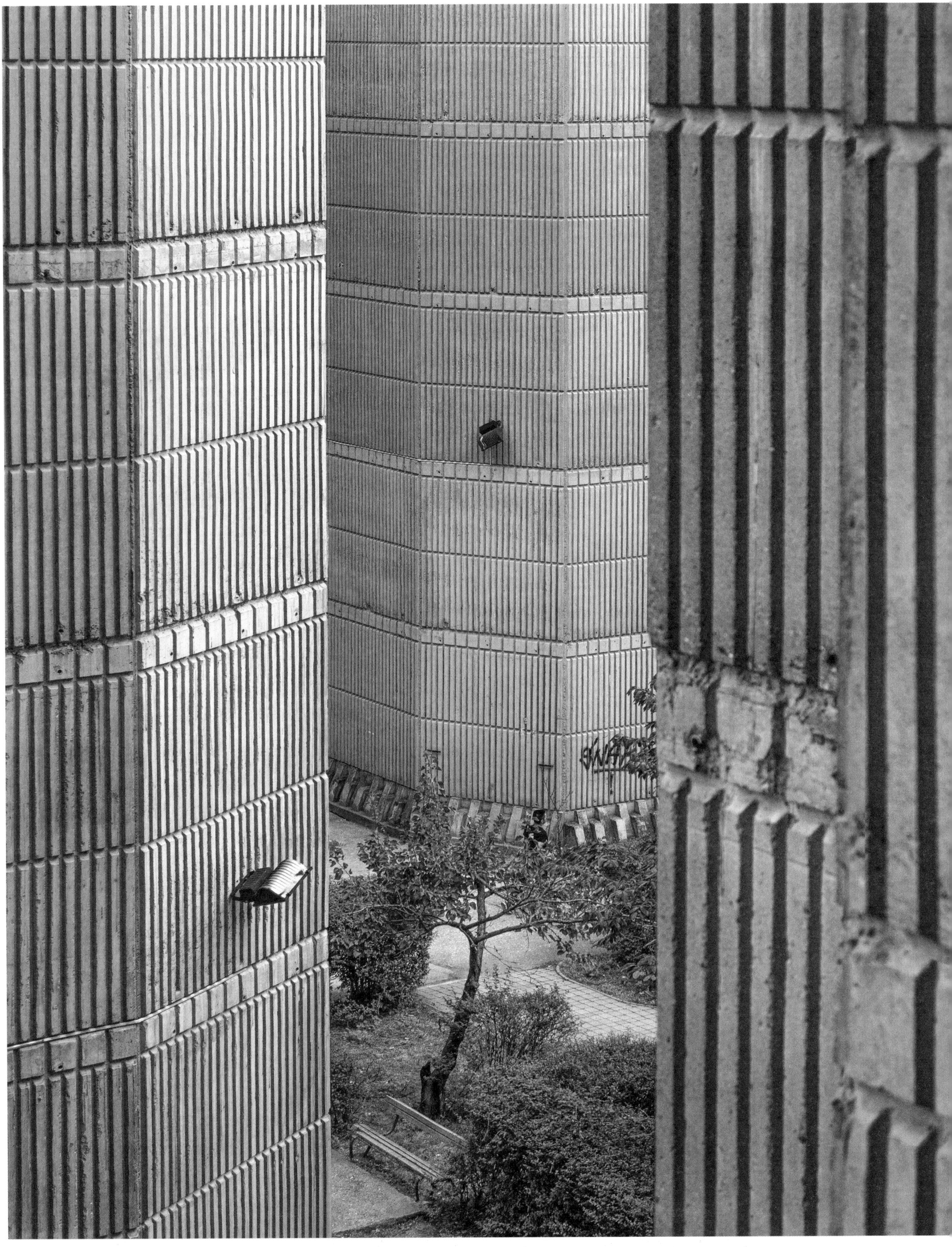

◁

The complex was designed by Georgi Konstantinovski, a pioneer of brutalist architecture in the Socialist Republic of Macedonia

△

Goce Delčev is the biggest dormitory in the country, accommodating over 120 students

functional bridge passages. There are also a smaller canteen block and sports facilities within the micro-estate. After the breakup of the Socialist Federal Republic of Yugoslavia, in 1992, the sizeable public constructions, like the 'Goce Delčev' dorm, and their expensive maintenance started to become a huge burden on the local government and they would be left to slowly deteriorate over the years. By the early 2000s the complex had become notorious for its bad living conditions. Students lacked basic amenities, such as hot water or central heating (aluminium foil would be stuck on the windows in an attempt to insulate the rooms from the cold) and the ceilings would leak when it rained heavily.

Given the 'Skopje 2014' campaign bashing the city's brutalist legacy over its mass neo-classical revival, it seemed, at one point, the future of Konstantinovski's design might not be bright. The recent general renovations carried out both in the building's exteriors and interiors completed in 2020 have however brought their modern character back to the constructions and they continue to impress to this day.

Otto-Braun-Straße
Berlin, Germany

Architects: M. Hörner, P. Senf, J. Härter
Built: 1968–1970

Complex of 4 concrete slabs
Currently abandoned

Berlin > Haus der Statistik

When walking around Alexanderplatz and its vicinity, one can almost sense the German Democratic Republic past pervading the present, leaving a strange feeling of what the Germans call 'ostalgia' – a nostalgia for the East German era. Indeed, since the German Unification in 1990, the area of East Berlin's central square with its iconic TV tower, erected in the 1960s, has remained a GDR relic. Its ostalgic character seems even more striking when mirrored with the West Berlin's Breitscheidplatz with steel and glass skyscrapers and a Mercedes star instead, symbolizing the 'other', capitalist world.

On the wave of the post-WWII reconstruction, a modernist plan for Alexanderplatz and the nearby streets was drafted by Joachim Näther and his team and by the 1970s edifices, such as the House of the Teacher, the House of Travel or the House of Statistics, rose on Alexanderstraße, Hans-Beimler-Straße (today Otto-Braun-Straße) and Stalinallee (today Karl-Marx Allee). Erected to house the GDR Central Administration of Statistics, Haus der Statistik is a large complex of four reinforced concrete buildings, ranging from two to 10 storeys. From the 1990s it was home to the Federal Statistical Office, and since

The facade of the abandoned Haus der Statistik became a canvas for many artistic interventions, such as the iconic 'Stop Wars'

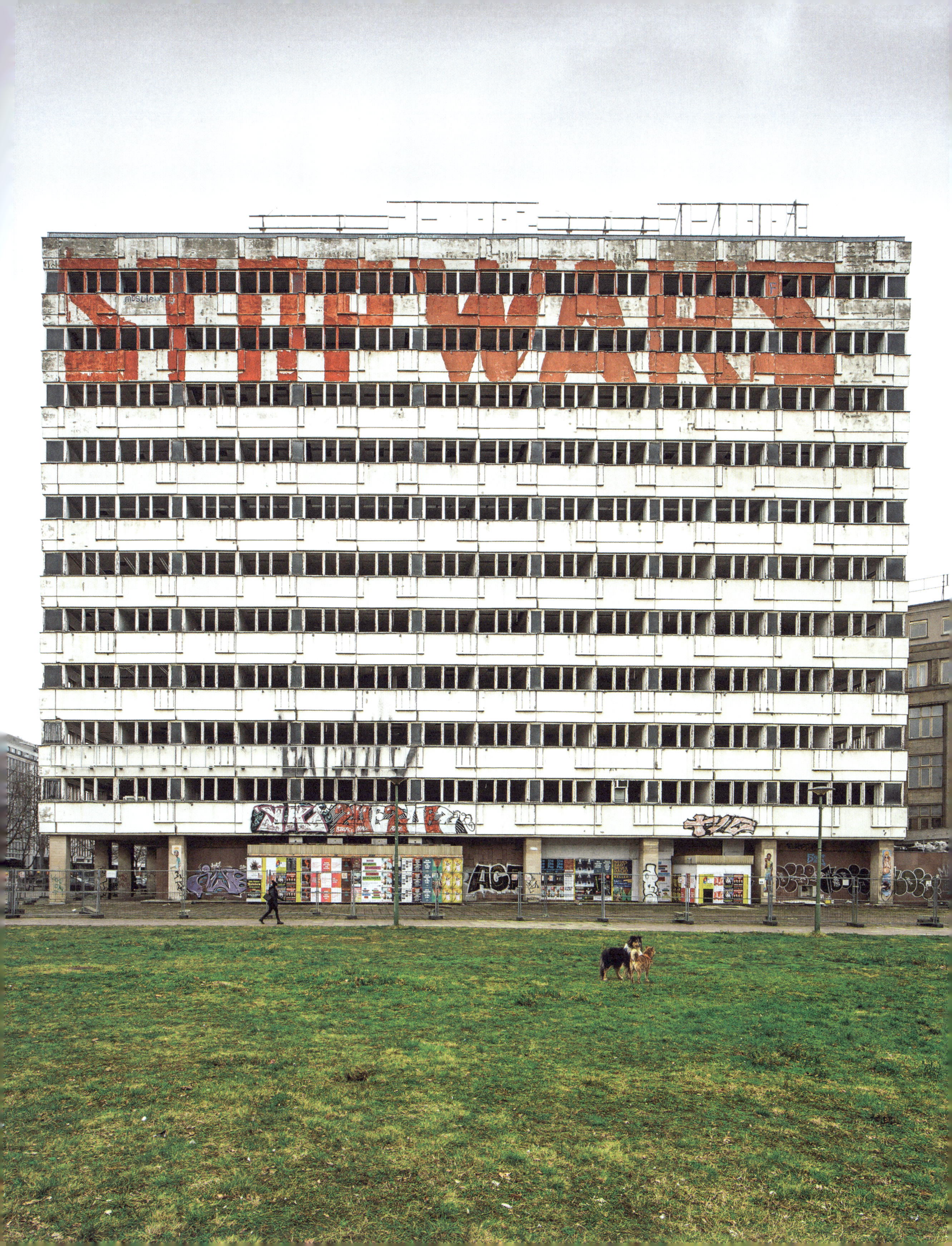
STOP WARS

△ Elevation details as seen from Otto-Braun-Straße

▷ The complex is a recognizable landmark of the former East Berlin's modernist city centre

2008 it has been abandoned. Similarly to the famous socialist realist mosaic 'Our Life' on the facade of the House of the Teacher, portraying the everyday life of a communist society, art also defined the final look of the House of Statistics. From the 'The History of Mathematics' educative five-part sculpture in front of the building and the impressive mural 'In Praise of Communism' in its interior, to the numerous artistic interventions, such as 'Stop Wars' or the 'Schrödinger's Cat' in recent years, the elevation of the abandoned building became an empty canvas taken over by Berliners to speak their mind through images and meaningful slogans.

Instead of its planned demolition that would allow the city to regain 45,000 m² of attractive Mitte district space, the complex is in for a complete renovation and hopefully at least part of it will be given at the people's disposal with affordable housing, art workshops and cultural centres for the local community.

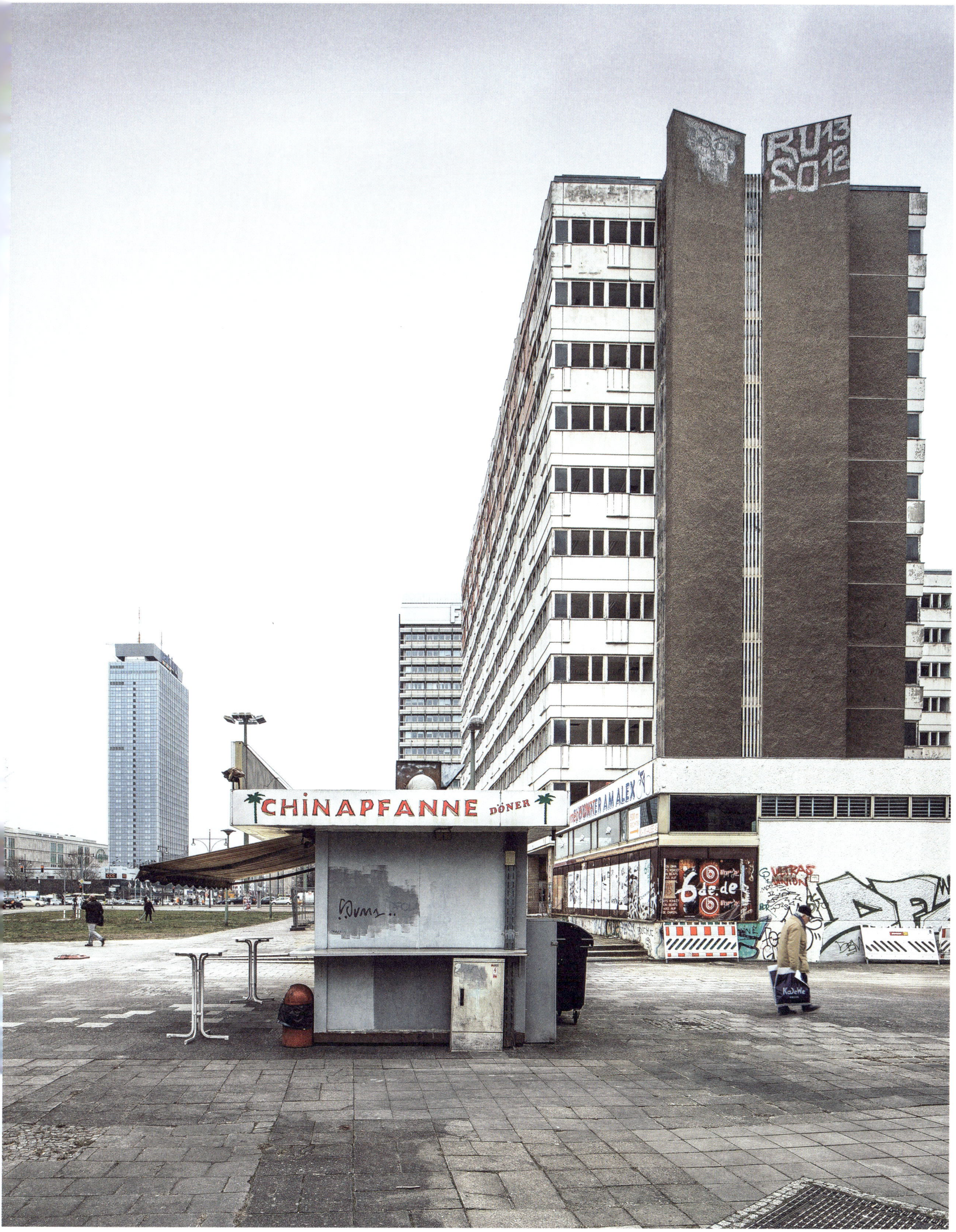
CHINAPFANNE DÖNER
RU 13
SO 12

District XVIII Architect: Csaba Virágh 140 housing blocks
Budapest, Hungary Built: 1977-1985 Prefab panel series 1-464A

Budapest > Havanna Housing Estate

Uniform fields of *panelház* were all you could see on the horizon of Budapest hinterlands in the 1970s. In response to a rapid growth of the city's population after WWII, the communist government drafted a five-year economic plan for Hungary which involved new housing for everyone. Following an experimental district of Óbuda – a seminal prefabricated panel micro-city built in the 1960s – 'house factories' quickly sprang up in other suburbs, giving rise to new concrete 'colonies' made of two types of prefabricated units – the Lars-Nielsen, originating in Denmark and commonly used to rebuild western European cities, and the Soviet large panel system type (LPS). Due to its functionality and affordability, the latter has monopolized the outskirts of Budapest for decades. The new *lakótelepek* (housing estates) were an assortment of different shapes, which could be assembled out of precast panels. High rises, slabs and concrete zigzags were copied from building type catalogues and pasted onto the urban landscape of the sleeping districts, such as Havanna, Újpalota or Csepel. The plan of the first one drafted by city architect Csaba Virágh was laid out in the virgin area of the southeastern suburb of Pest, incorporated into the city only in the 1950s and transformed into Pestszentlőrinc,

Colourful patterns present on the *panelház's* elevations help to tell the blocks apart

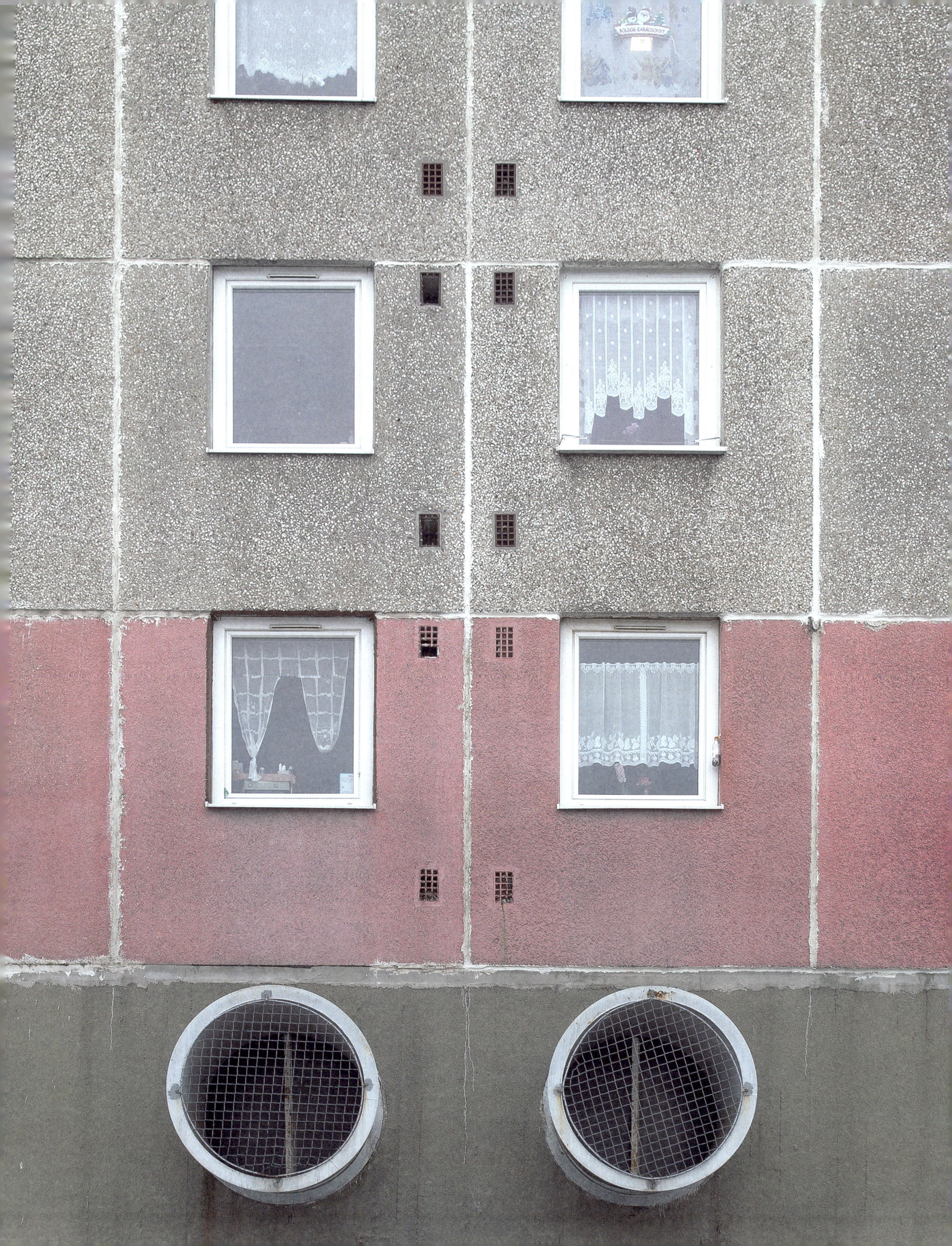

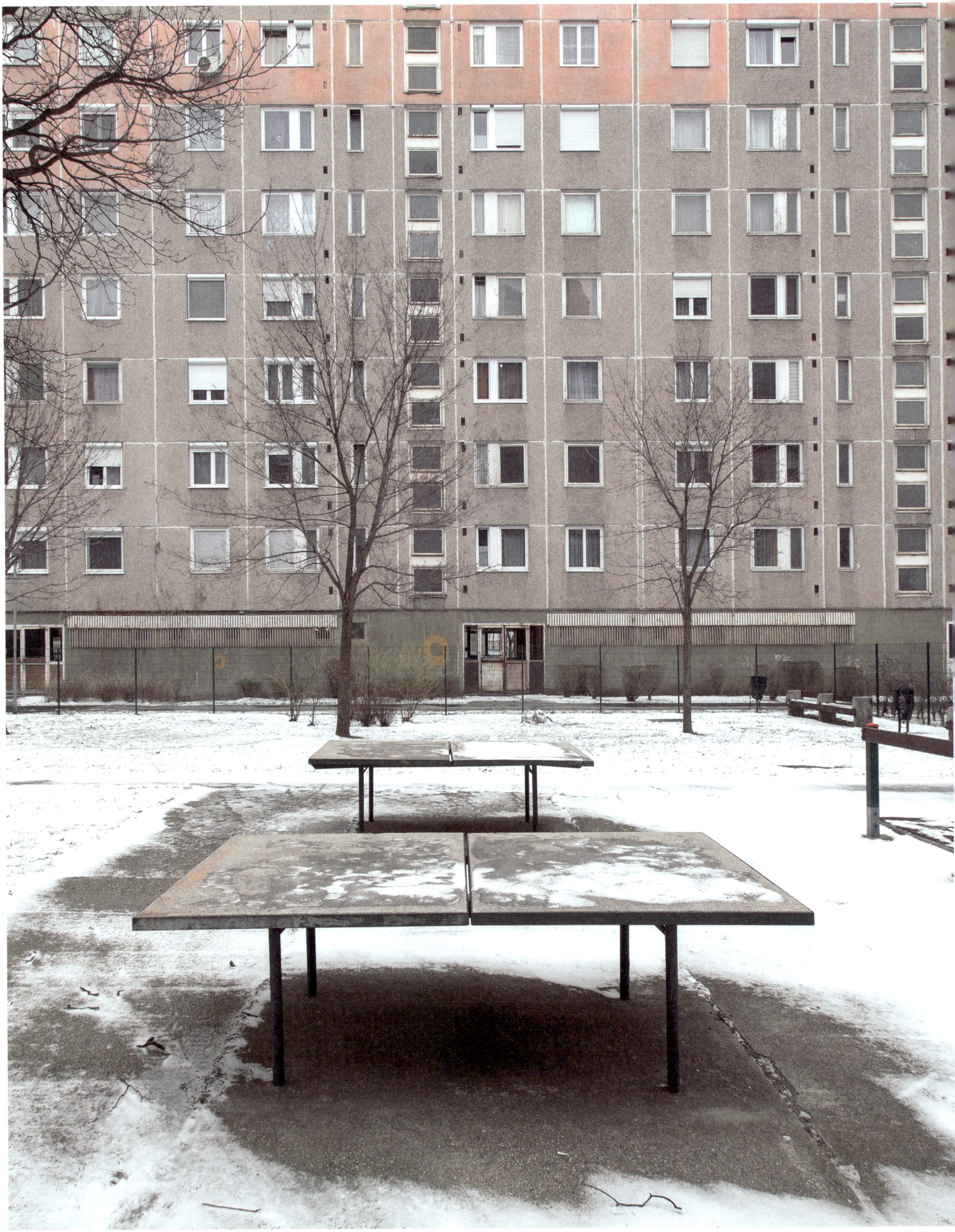

◁

A playground between panel block rows in Barta Lajos street

△

Csepel-Erdőalja housing estate in District XXI

part of District XVIII. Havanna grew slowly but steady. Over 6,000 homes for 20,000 people were erected over two construction rounds, from 1977 to 1981 and from 1983 to 1985, out of the 1-464A prefab panel series and its variants developed by the Central Scientific and Research Institute for Experimental Design (TsNIIEP) in Russia and imported to Hungary. A number of 10-storey blocks were arranged in four symmetrical rows intertwined with greenery and playgrounds, mirroring one another on both sides of the central area where a school, kindergarten, shops and a cultural centre are located. Unlike in other former Eastern Bloc countries where the vast majority of mass housing was state owned, here private ownership was allowed and the estate was partially managed by housing cooperatives, while those who rented the council apartments could apply for acquiring them after a circa 20-year period.

Although the reputation of the estate had been quite shattered in the 1990s, the LPS houses have recently become popular among young families who appreciate the suburban locality with all the necessary facilities just round the corner, a socialist dream come true.

Viery Charužaj street
Minsk, Belarus

Architect: Vladimir Pushkin
Built: 1969 -1997

5 residential tower blocks
16 storeys each

Minsk > 'Kukuruza' Housing Complex

The post-war history of Minsk is one of a city wiped away and rebuilt from scratch on the ruins of its traditional wooden houses and Baroque churches. The new capital was remade out of concrete moulded into all kinds of forms: geometrical, streamlined, and otherworldly, shaping one of the most intriguing Soviet skylines in the entire USSR. Designed in the late 1960s on the socialist modernist wave, Kukuruza ('corn' in Belarusian) tower blocks were the ultimate avant-garde interpretation of collective housing in Minsk. The five 16-storey houses would rise one by one over a period of two decades along Viery Charužaj street in Saviecki District, puzzling the Minskians with their unusual shapes, resembling the design of Kyiv's Obolon towers. Indeed, being the first buildings in Belarus erected out of frame technology, their construction was so novel, even their designer Vladimir Potershchuk of 'Belgosproekt' (the National Design Institute of the Republic of Belarus) found this project extremely challenging. In order to achieve the signature 'corn' look, which won the architects a third prize at the Exhibition of Achievements of the National Economy in Moscow, customized rounded balcony panels needed to be developed

The last 'corn' on the intersection of Viery Charužaj and Kujbyšava streets, with Komarovsky market on the right

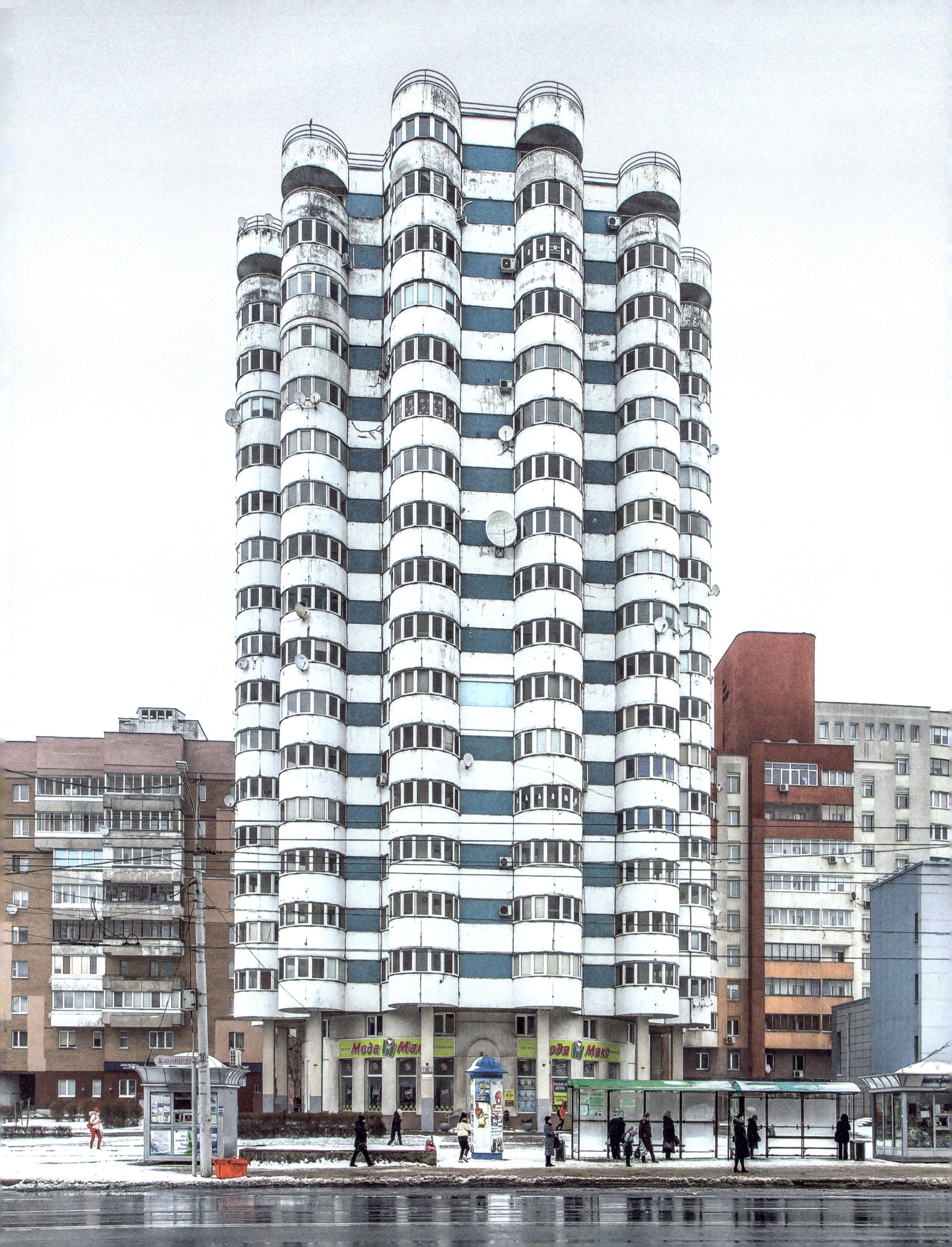

and manufactured from scratch. Although the skyscrapers seem identical on the outside, there are some differences visible only to those who can access their interiors. Due to considerable time intervals between the construction of the towers, their various investors decided to arrange the flats according to their own visions of each 'cob'. In general, however, those who were granted homes here could boast spacious flats unparalleled to any other location in Minsk in the Brezhnev era, including duplex apartments, now transformed into offices. The inhabitants ranged from ordinary 'proletariat' citizens, who came into possession of their homes through a long waiting list, to business people and celebrities who would spend significant rubles to purchase their apartments in the last 'cob'. With a concierge, new lifts and parking lot right outside, the last Kukuruza, completed in 1997, is known as the 'elite' tower.

△
Almost identical residential tower blocks were erected in 1981 in Obolonskyi District of Kyiv, Ukraine

▷
The tower blocks were the first buildings in Belarus built using frame technology and their construction required special oval panels

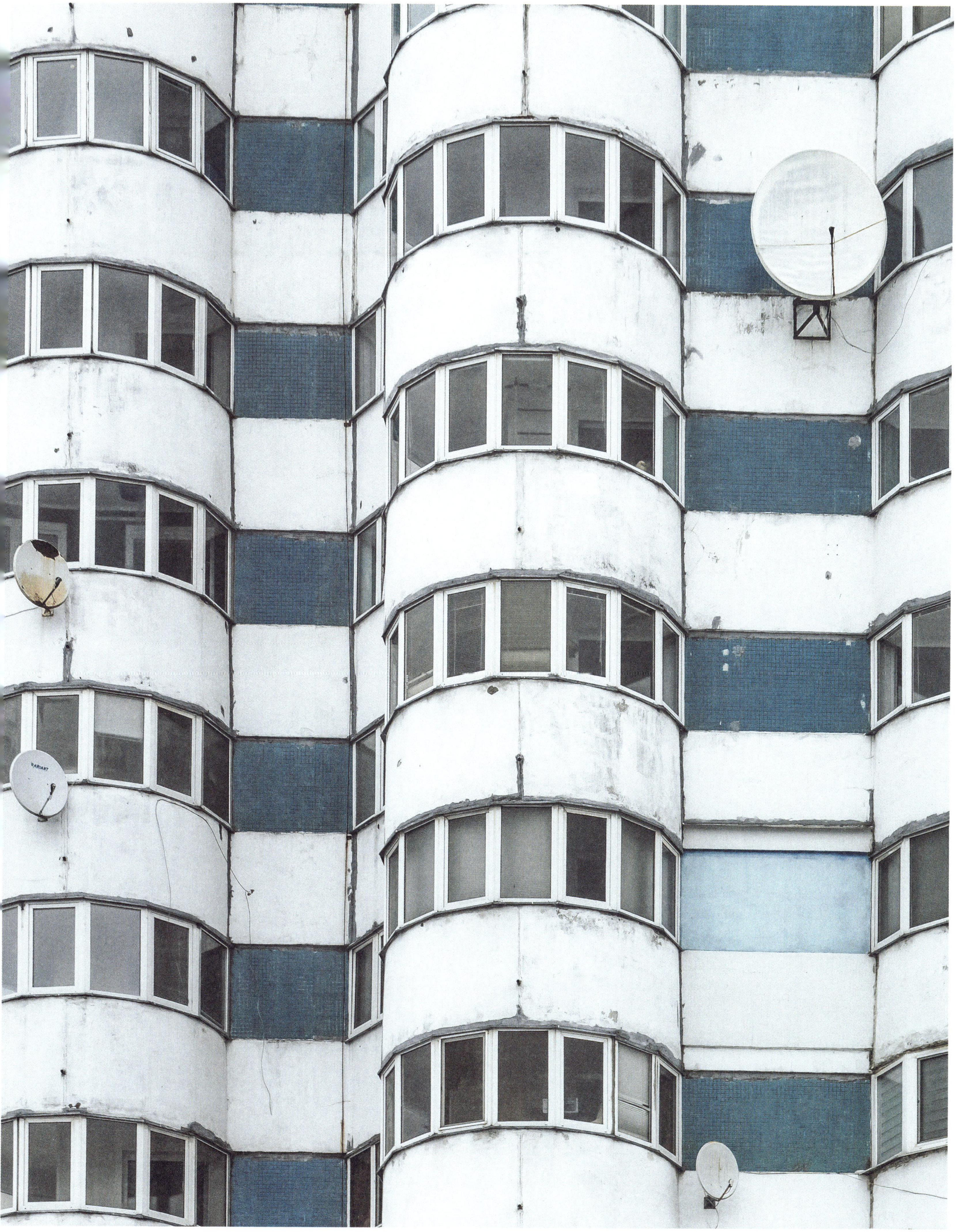

A155, Dombay
Karachay-Cherkess Republic, Russia

Architects: G. Kostomarov, E. Perchenkov
Built: 1980

480 rooms
Currently abandoned

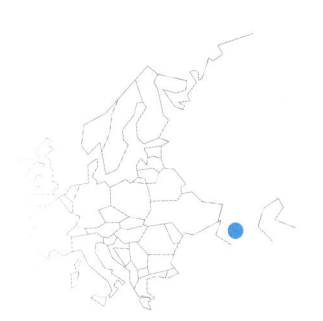

Dombay > Hotel Amanauz

Situated at the foot of the Caucasus Mountains amidst the Teberda Nature Reserve lies a small holiday settlement – Dombay. Administratively part of the Karachay-Cherkess Republic, bordering Georgia, the ski resort became popular among winter sport fans in the early 1930s and by the 1960s developed a fully-fledged tourist infrastructure with hotels, ski lifts and all sorts of amenities for visitors. Over the next few decades, Dombay grew outwards and upwards, and aspired to become a location for the more demanding Russian clientele.

The bold design drawn up by Perchenkov and Kostomarov of the Central Scientific and Research Institute for Experimental Design in Moscow (TsNIIEP) in the early 1980s was a crucial part of this plan. The new hotel was to provide accommodation for over 600 guests, and house a cinema, cafe, concert hall and other 'luxury' facilities, while its brutalist geometrical body with wooden panels clad on top of the raw concrete and characteristic checkerboard balconies resembling ski lift cabins resonate with the environment. Construction began in 1980 and was planned to be completed within five years. However, in 1985, all works ceased and the hotel has been left unfinished and abandoned ever since. Rumour has it that the building was to be placed on a platform rotating the building with the speed of the sun around its axis, and most likely it was the extravagant foundation plans gone wrong that killed this intriguing project before it fully materialized. The mighty tower block nonetheless remains the highest edifice in Dombay and despite its derelict state today, it still inspires awe with its grandeur and boldness.

The hotel's balconies resembling ski lift cabins or honeycombs

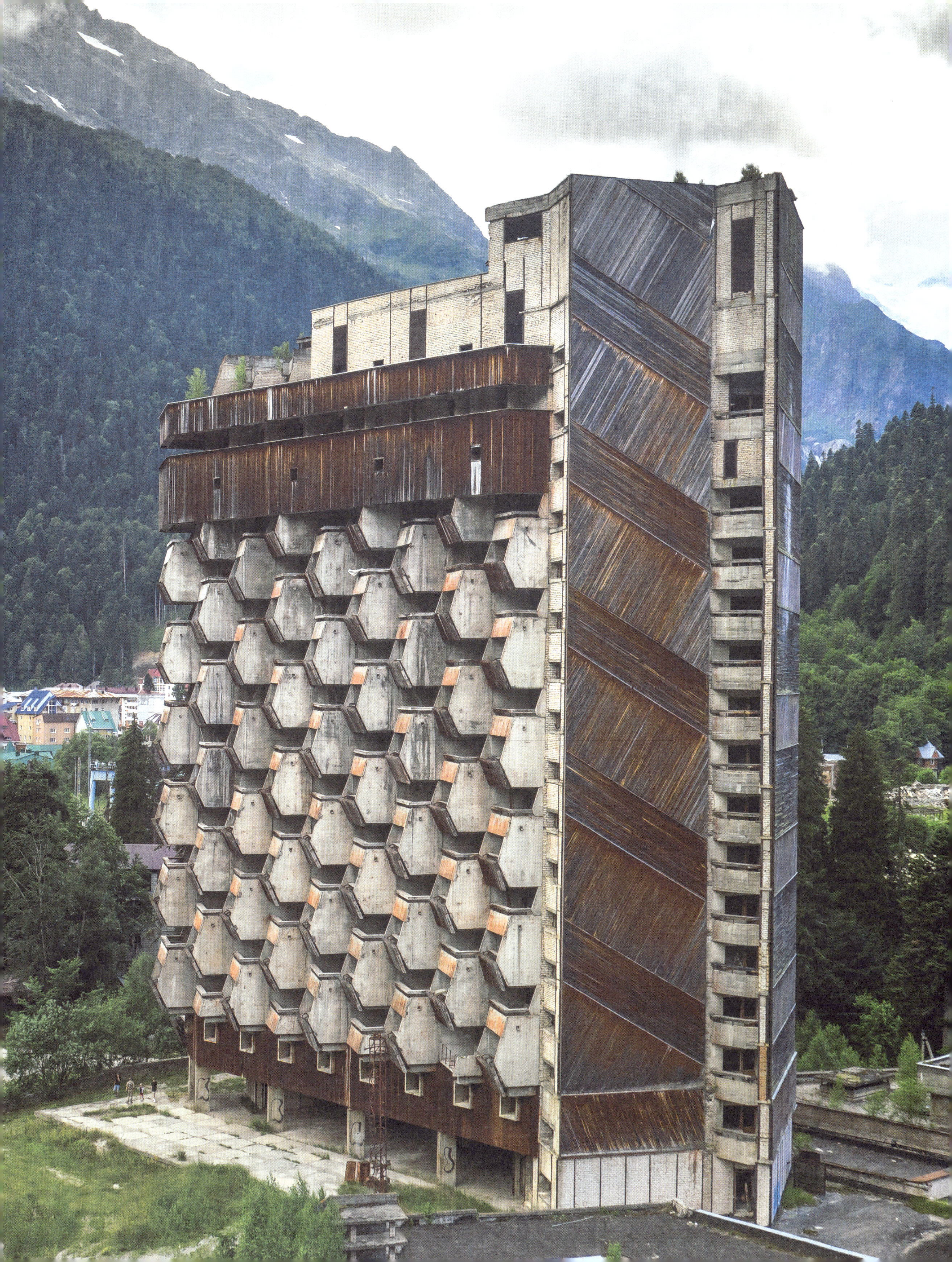

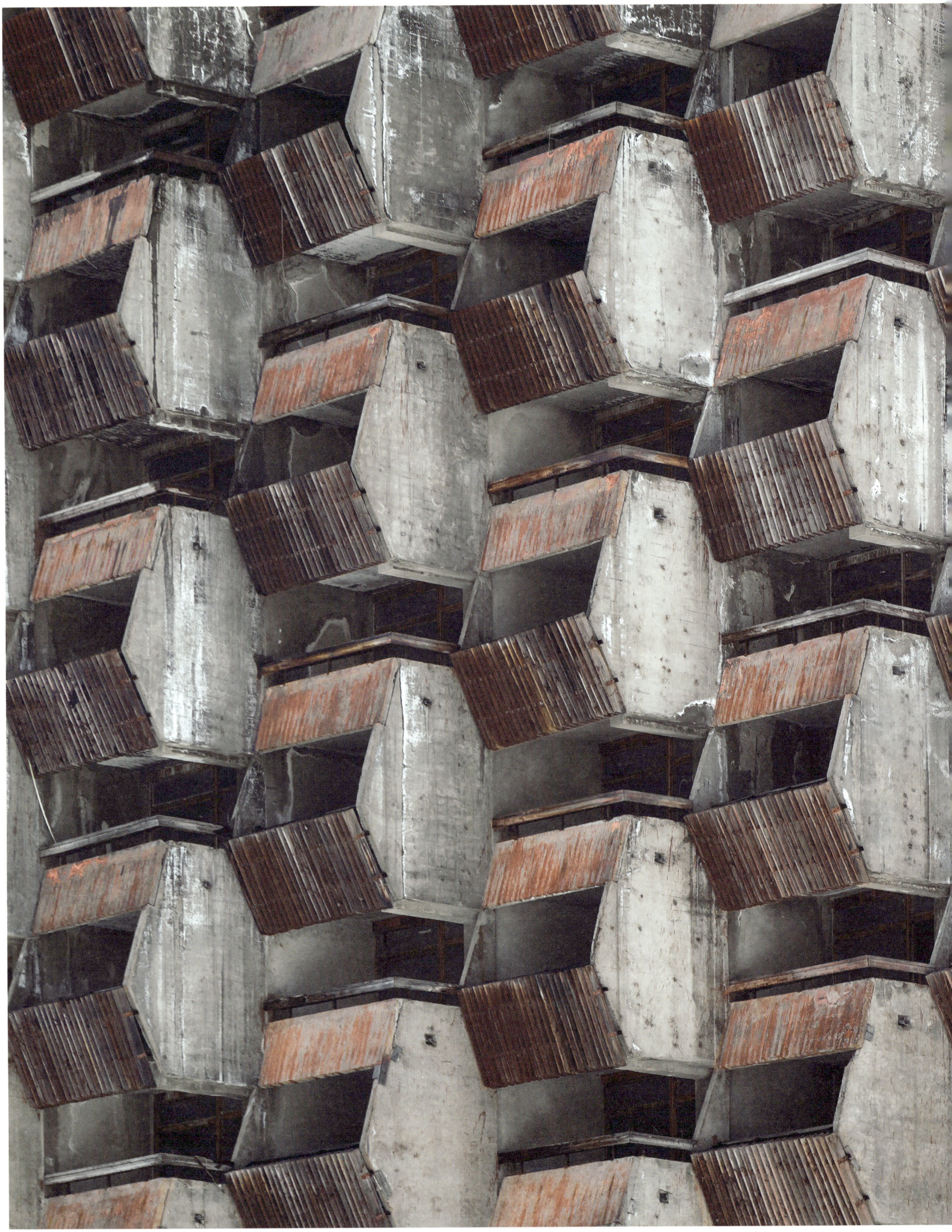

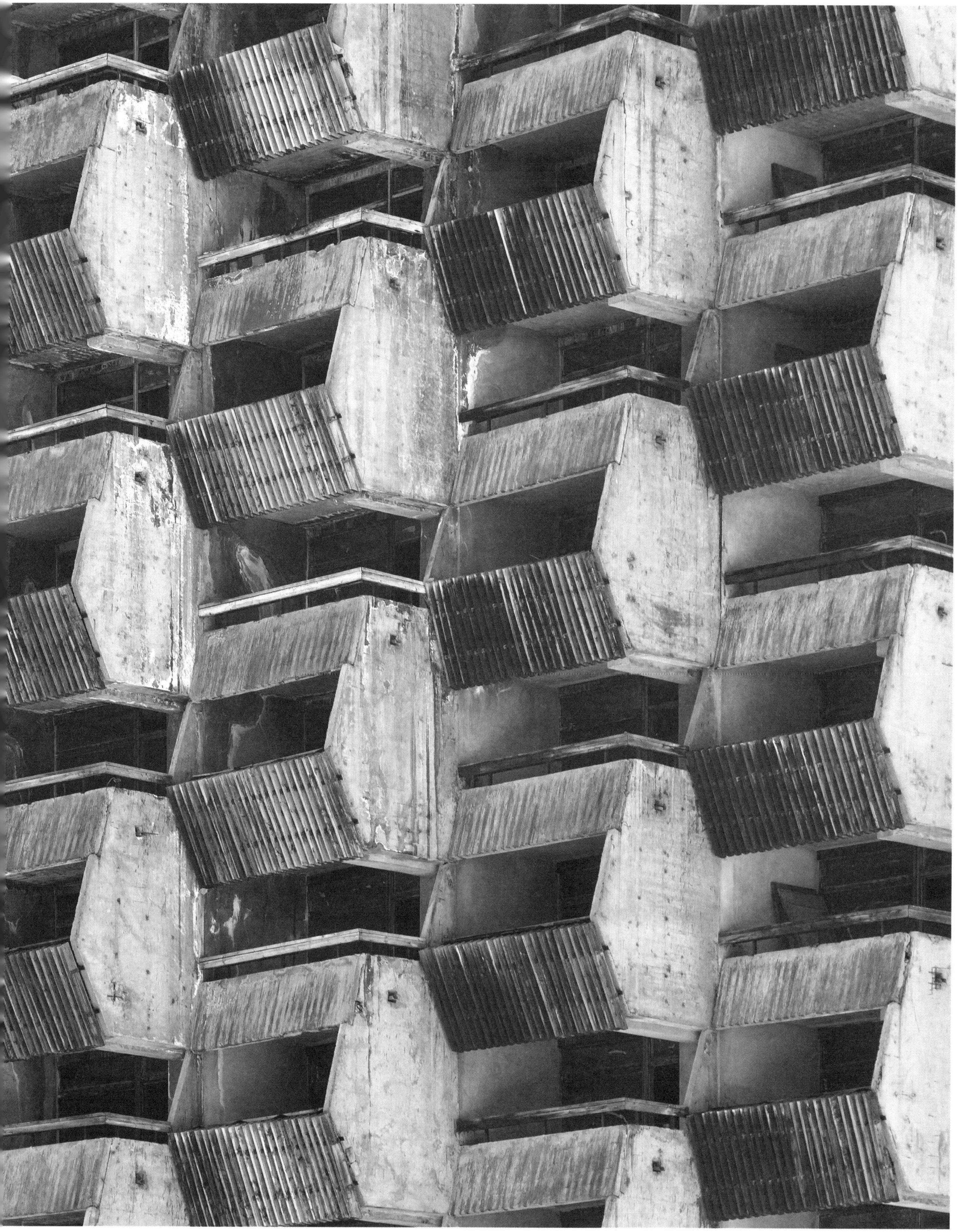

Buzludzha Peak
Kazanluk, Bulgaria

Architect: Georgi Stoilov
Built: 1974-1981

Memorial House
Currently abandoned

Buzludzha > The Monument House of the Bulgarian Communist Party

A striking edifice resembling a flying saucer with a raw concrete monolith behind towers above the limestone and granite Hadzhi Dimitar peak in the Central Balkan Mountains. The memorial and event venue, erected between 1974 and 1981, following the design of Georgi Stoilov, is certainly one of the most breath-taking pieces of brutalist architecture worldwide. From the battle with the Ottoman Turks to the foundation of the Bulgarian Social Democratic Workers Party under Dimitâr Blagoev in 1891, and finally the 1944 fight between the communist partisans and the Bulgarian Army, the peak, better known as Buzludzha, has witnessed some breakthrough historical moments. Built for the people and by the people (the construction was founded with private donations and built by 6,000 workers, including volunteers, engineers, designers, artists and soldiers), it was to commemorate the birth of a socialist nation. Over only eight years of its lifespan, circa three million visitors made a pilgrimage to this communist temple before it was closed down in 1989 following the political transformation that embraced the entire Eastern Bloc. Stoilov's design took from inverse architectural genres, such as futurism

The monument is made up of two structures, the UFO-shaped main body and concrete 70-m high tower with the red star on top

НА КРАК
О ПАРИИ ПРЕЗРЕНИ
ПОТИСНАТИ И УНИЖЕНИ
РАБОТНИЦИ
РАБОТНИЧКИ

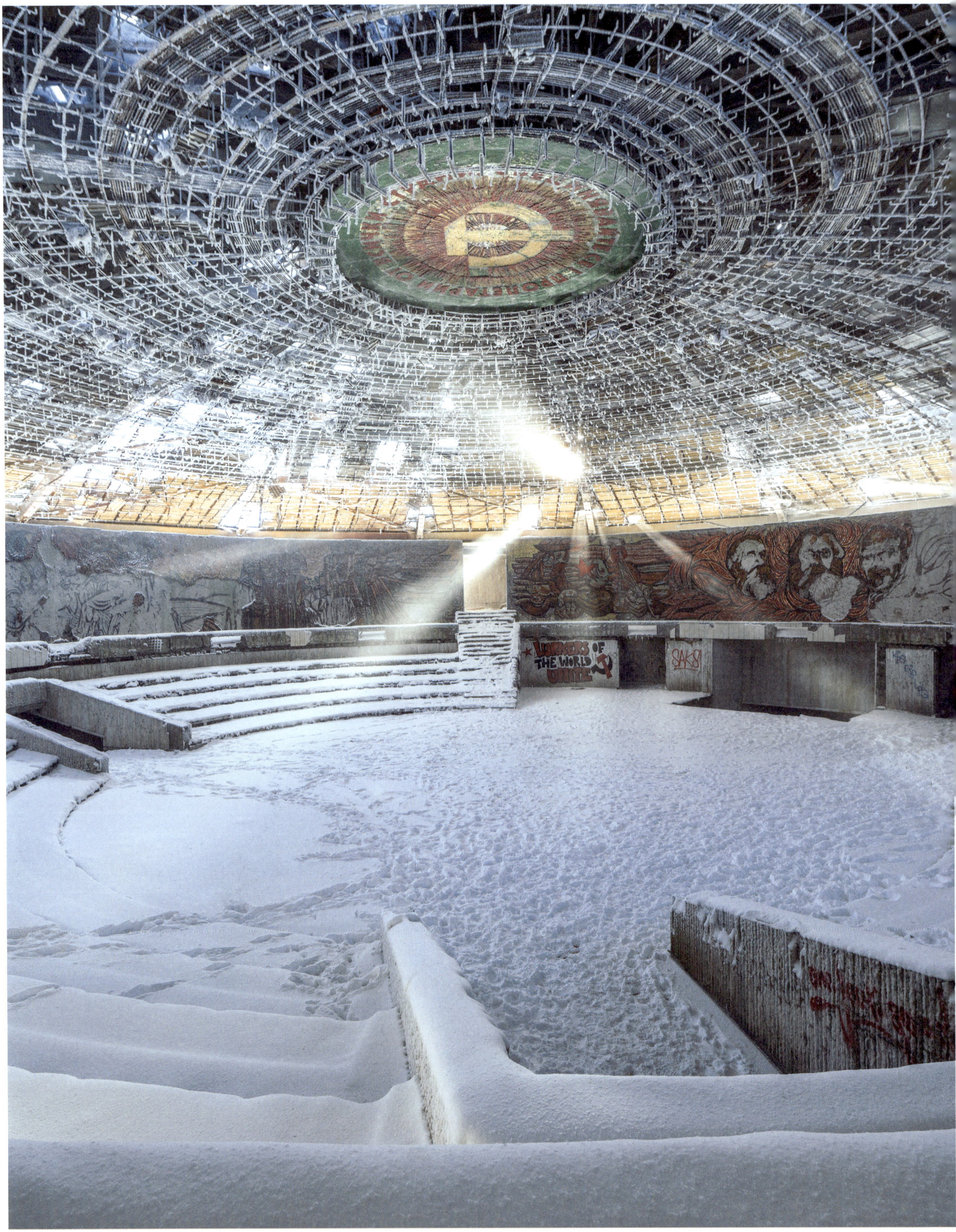
OF
THE WORLD
SAK8

and classicism. Cosmic on the outside, the oval shape symbolizes infinity while the interior was meant to resemble the Roman Pantheon, but with the hammer and sickle accompanied with the communist slogan 'Proletarians of all countries, unite!' at the core of the dome.

The central arena was surrounded with 510 m² of spectacular mosaic artwork created by over 20 Bulgarian artists, ornamented with red stars and the busts of Marx, Engels and Lenin alongside Bulgarian communist leaders and figures of people of all walks of life overlooking the auditorium. These were transformed into accidental modern collages with graffiti painted all around when in the late 1990s the building was left unguarded. Decades of vandalism and harsh winters with temperatures falling to −20 degrees Celsius left Buzludzha in rack and ruin and, more so after the 2016 decommunization bill passed in Bulgaria, imposing restrictions on communist symbols in public space, it seemed like its decay had reached a point of no return. In 2019, however, the monument had a lucky break and was awarded a Getty Foundation grant which is to fund its renovation. Whether the works commenced at the end of 2020 will undo the harm it has suffered for so long remains to be seen.

◁
The mosaics take up over 500 m2 of the building's interior and are composed of over two million pieces. Only 50% of the original artwork survived to this day

△
'Workers - men and women of the world - unite! Ahead! Comrades, let's bravely build up our great cause! Let's work, let's create - the worker to enlighten!' – says the inscription near the entrance

—

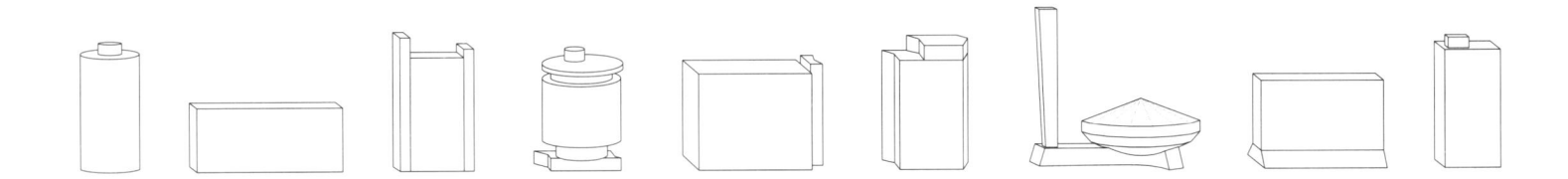

Models are die-cut and pre-folded

Carefully press all elements out

Firmly fold all parts before assembling

White glue is recommended

Enjoy!

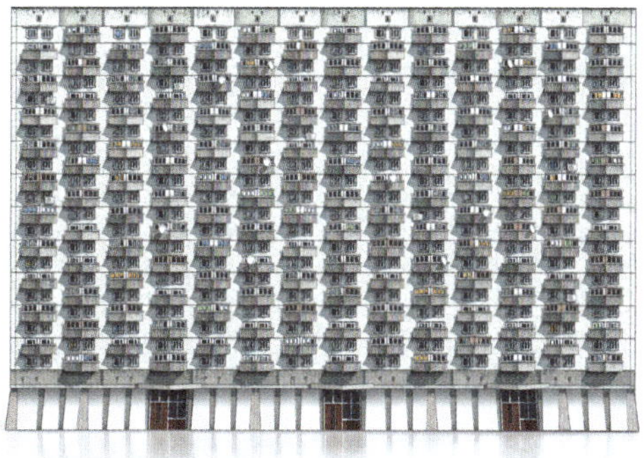

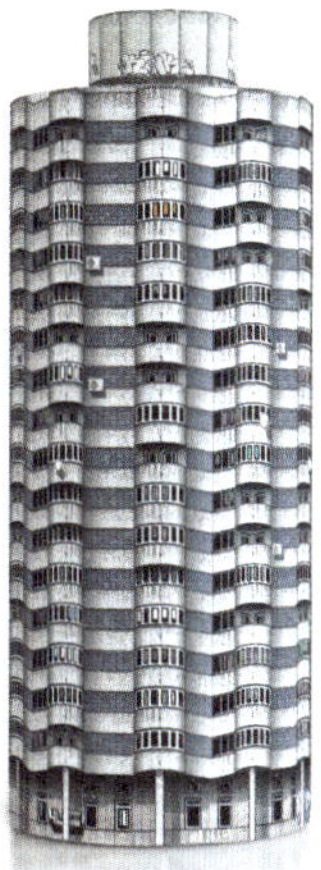

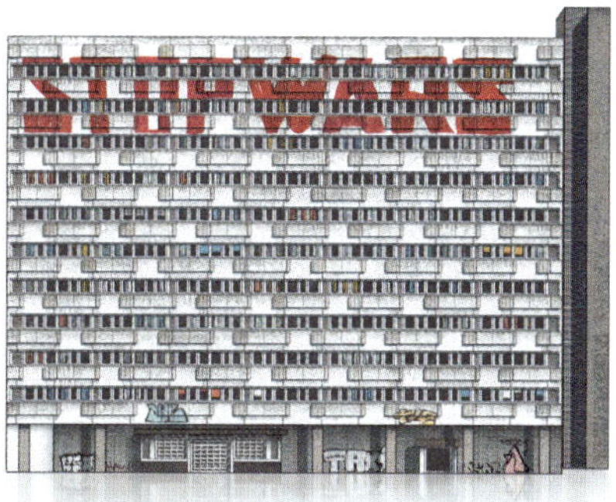

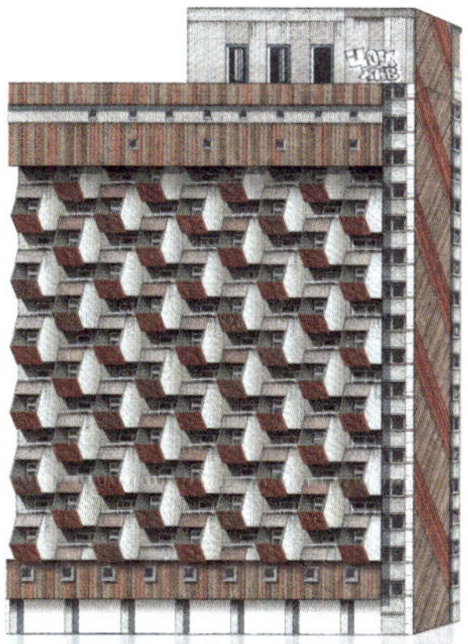

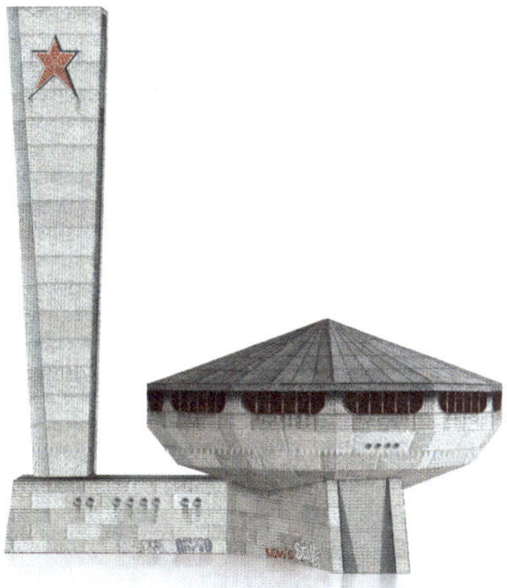

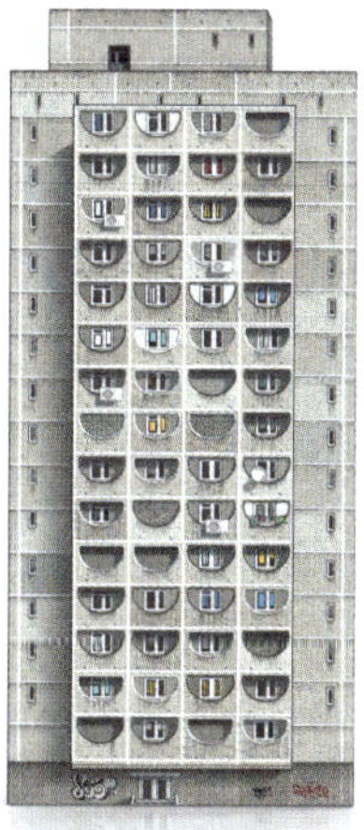

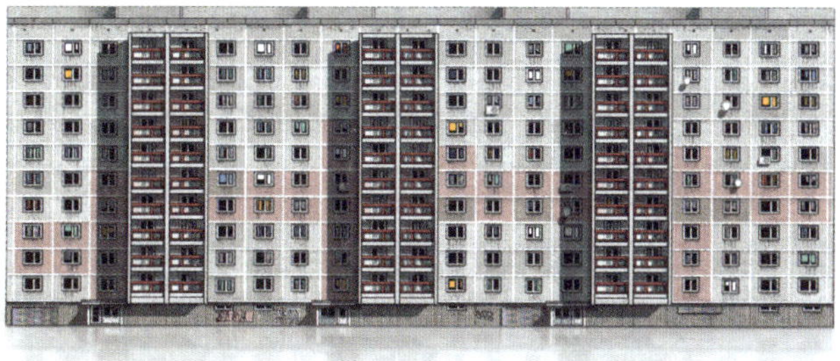

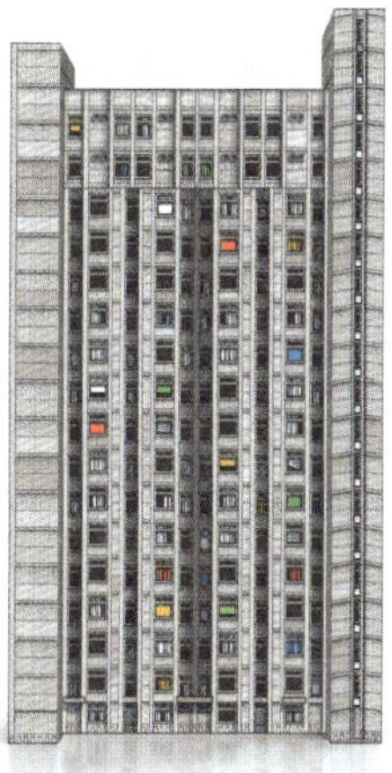

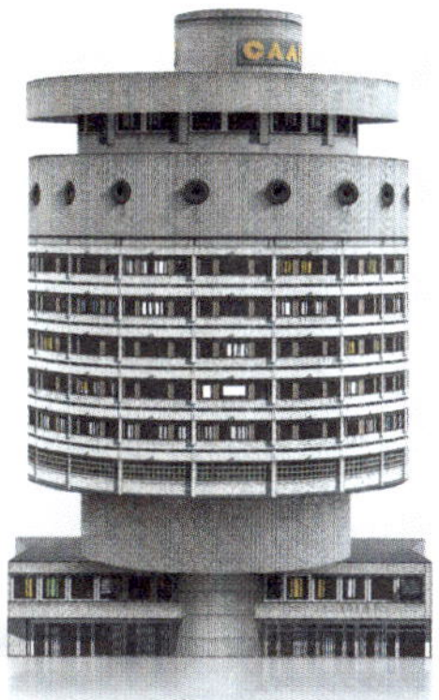

Moscow 'The House on Chicken Legs'

by Zupagrafika

Tbilisi 'Sky-Bridge' Housing Estate

by Zupagrafika

Kyiv Hotel Salute

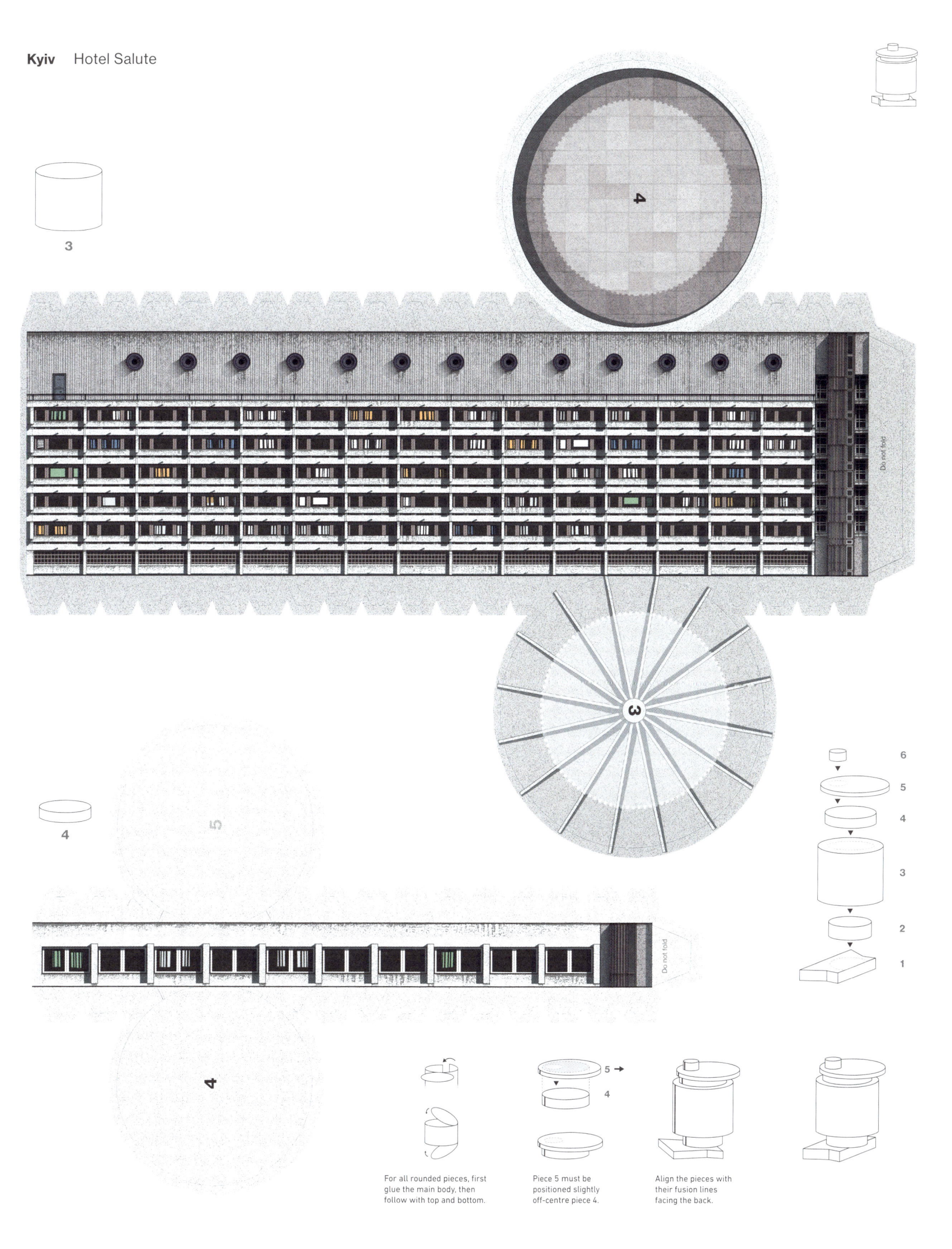

For all rounded pieces, first glue the main body, then follow with top and bottom.

Piece 5 must be positioned slightly off-centre piece 4.

Align the pieces with their fusion lines facing the back.

Kyiv Hotel Salute

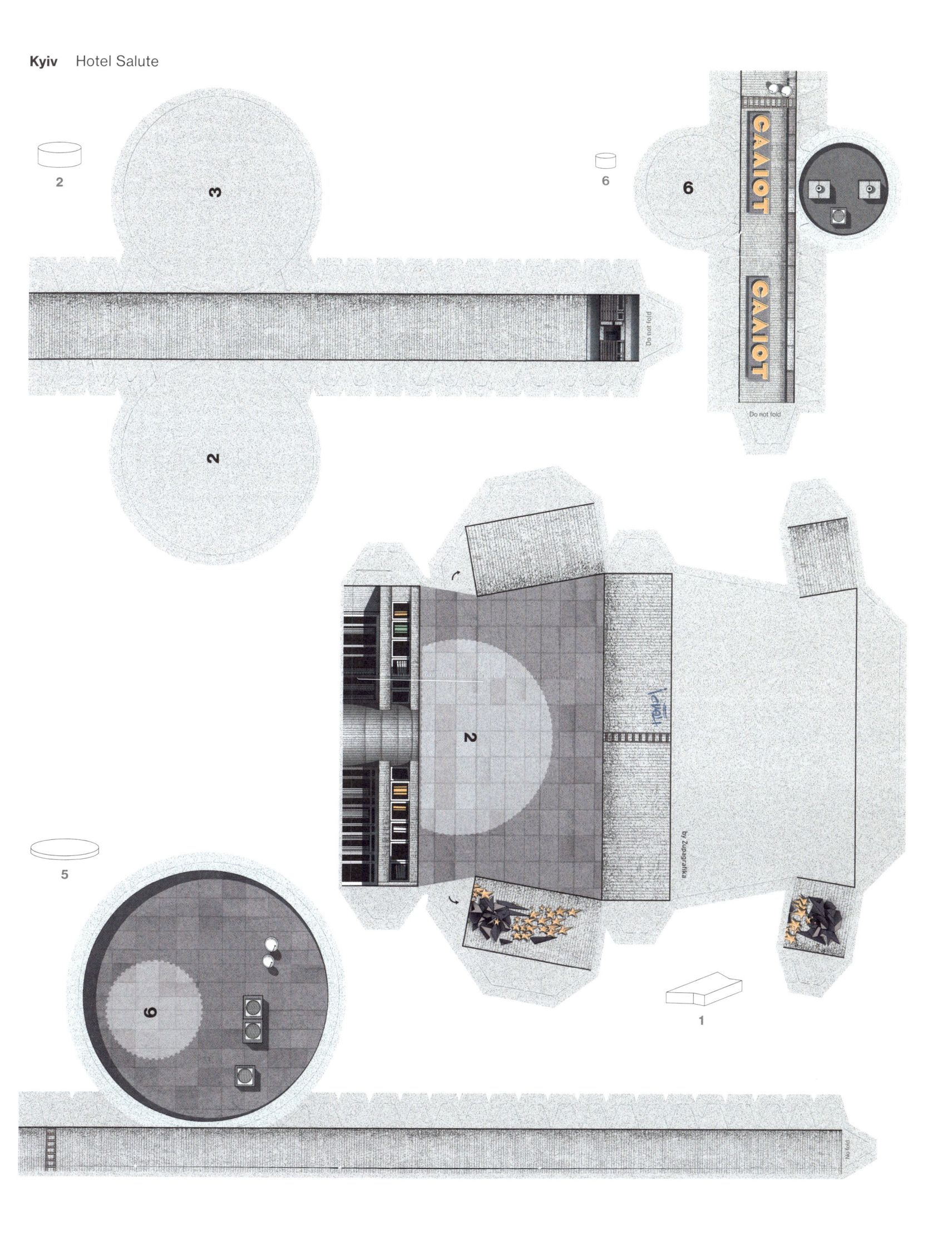

Skopje Studentski Dom 'Goce Delčev'

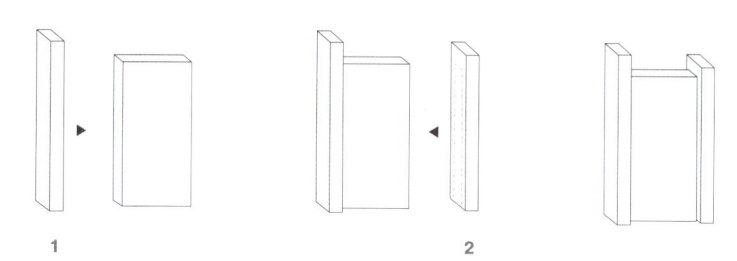

Skopje Studentski Dom 'Goce Delčev'

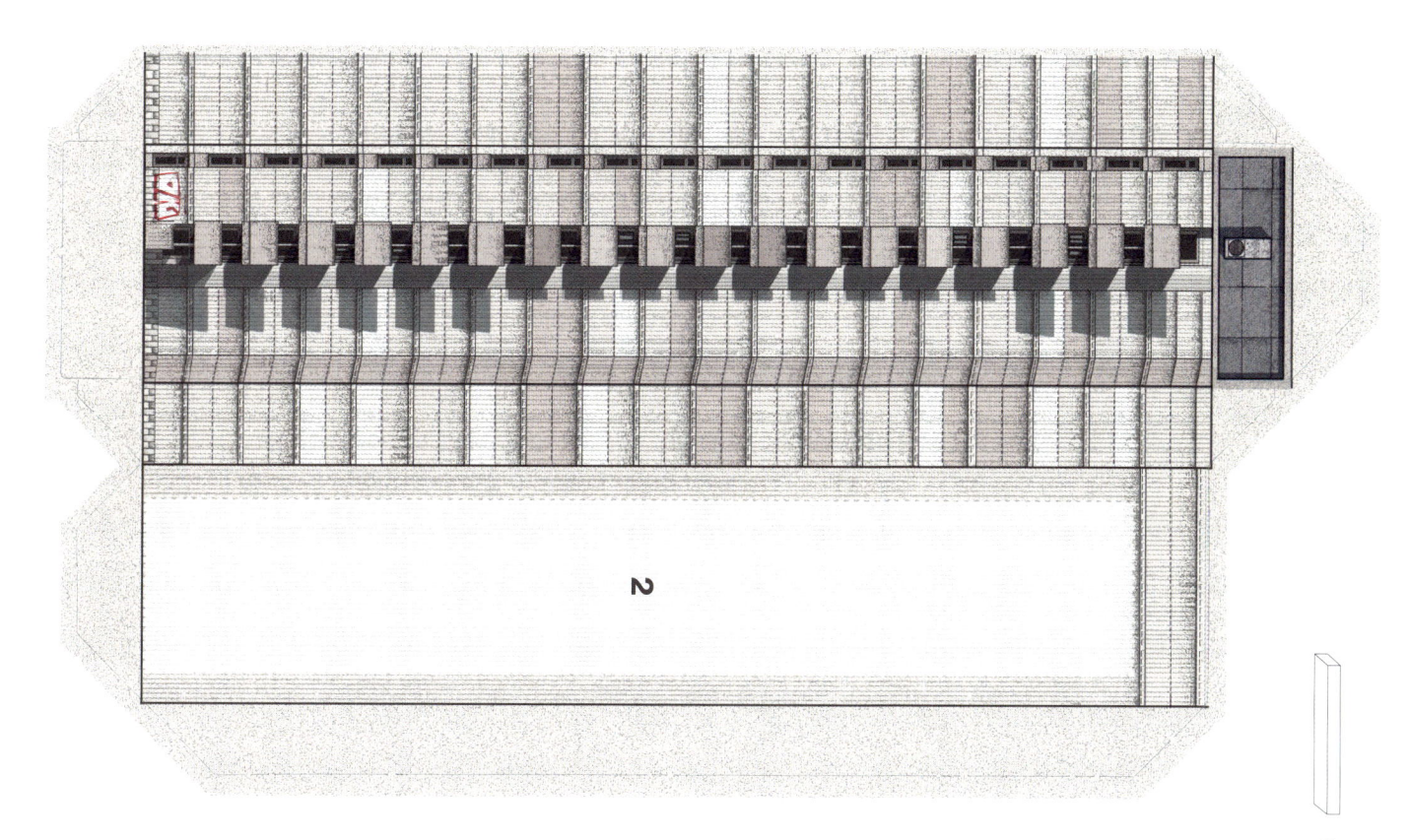

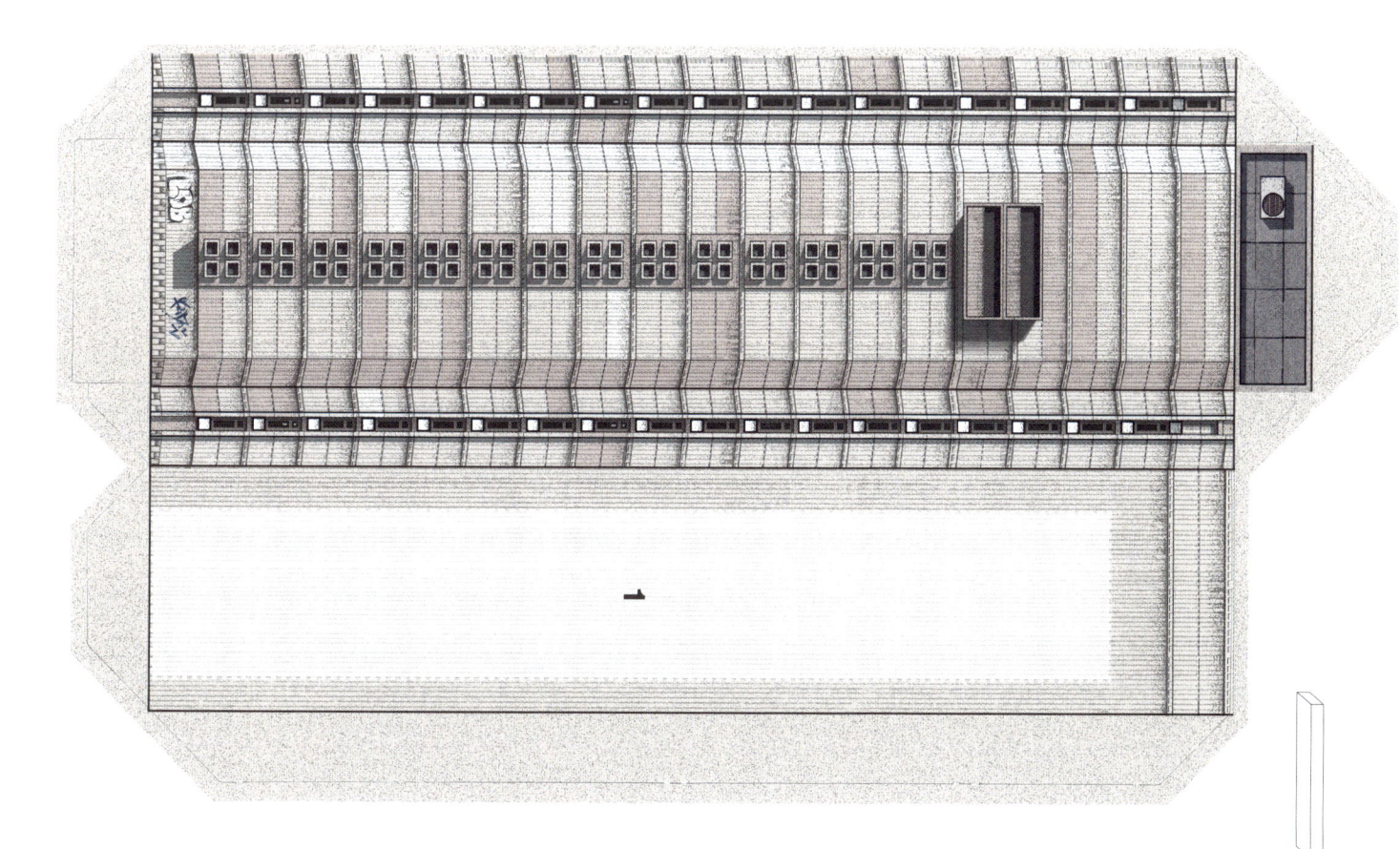

Berlin Haus der Statistik

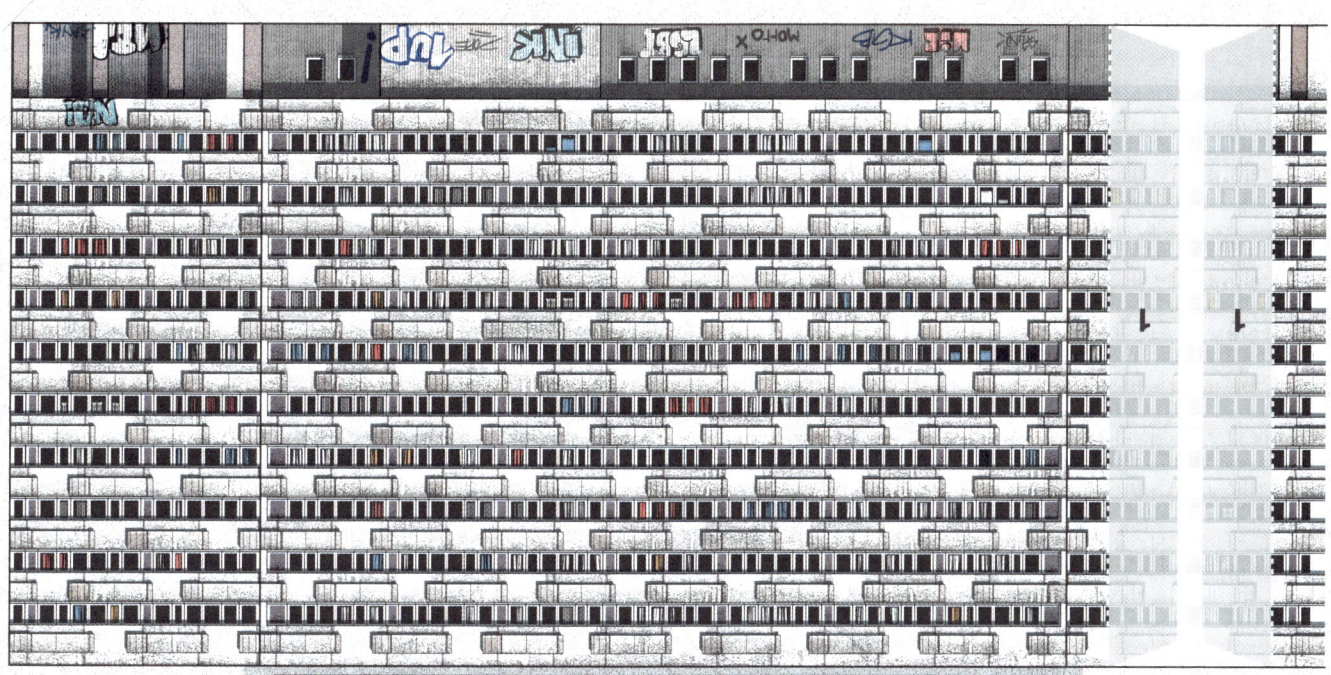

Budapest Havanna Housing Estate

Minsk 'Kukuruza' Housing Complex

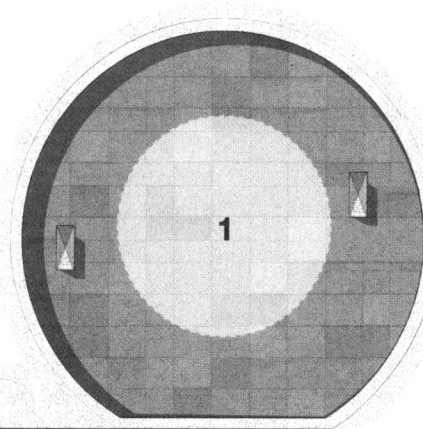

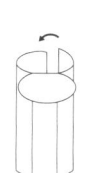

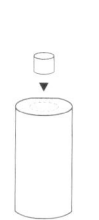

Dombay
Hotel Amanauz

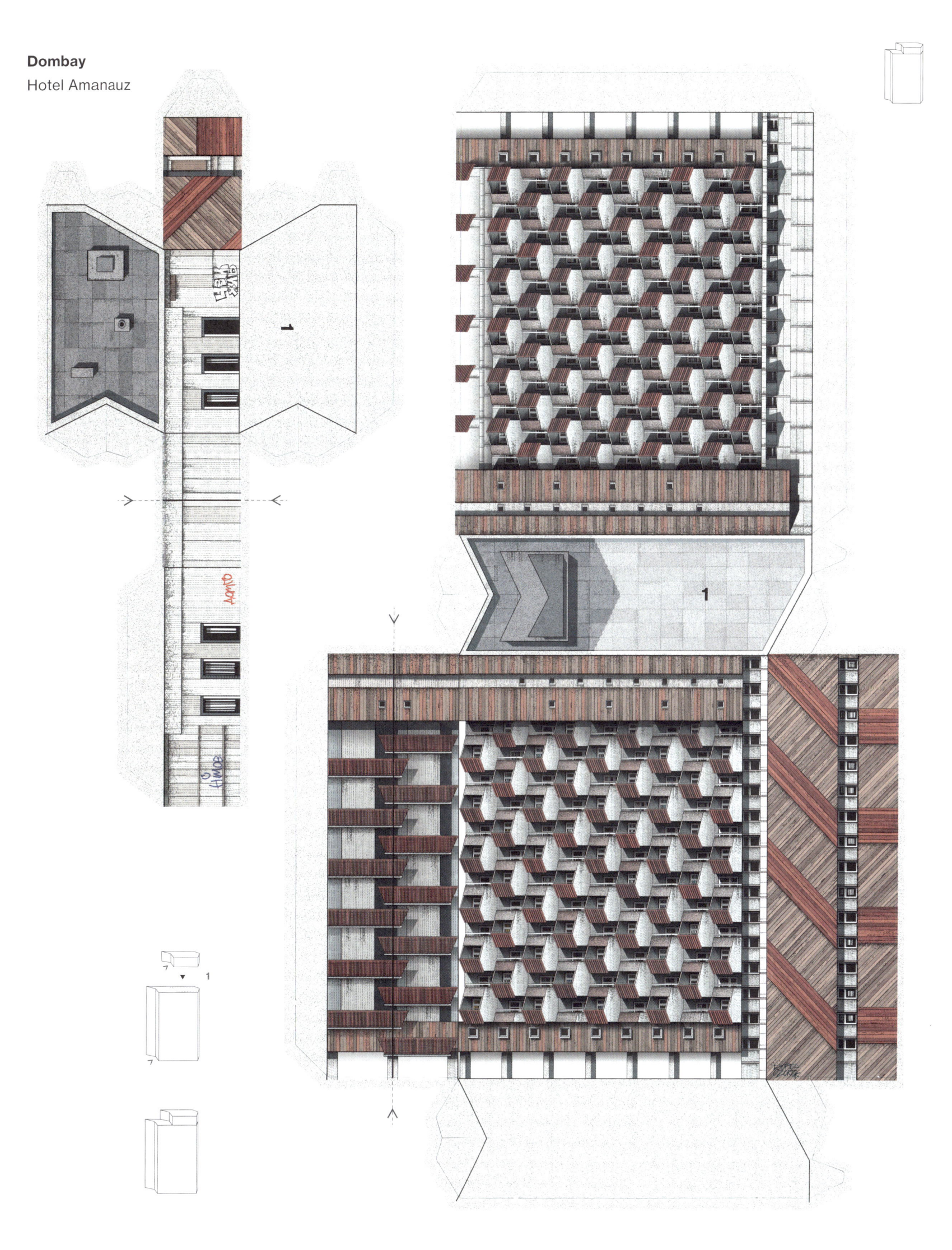

Buzludzha
The Monument House of the BCP

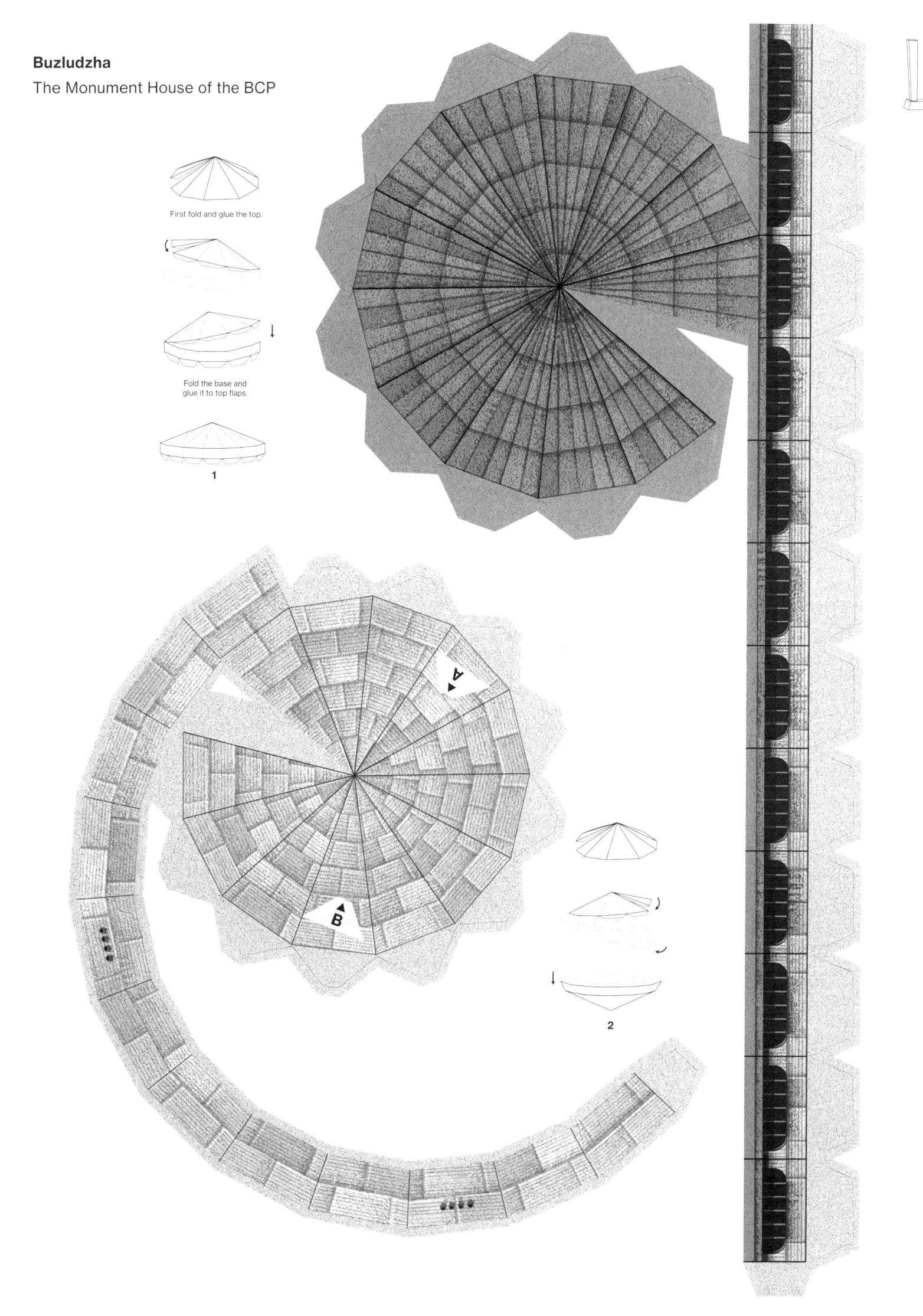

First fold and glue the top.

Fold the base and glue it to top flaps.

1

2

Buzludzha

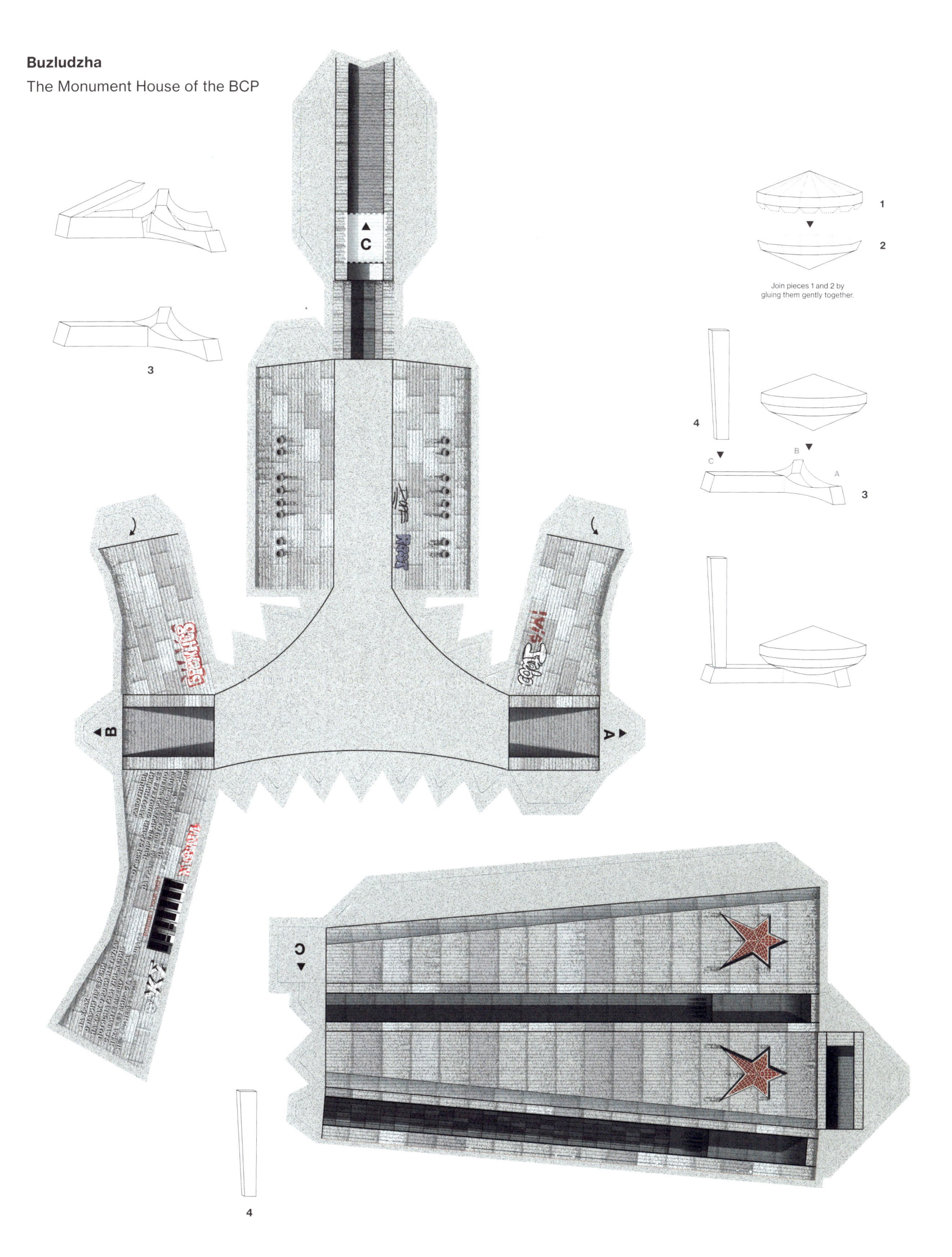

The Monument House of the BCP

Join pieces 1 and 2 by gluing them gently together.

Author

Zupagrafika are David Navarro and Martyna Sobecka, an independent publisher, author and graphic design studio, established in 2012 in Poznań, Poland, celebrating modernist architecture, design and photography in a unique and playful way.

Over the last decade, David and Martyna have created, illustrated and published award-winning books exploring the brutalist and post-war modernist architecture of the former Eastern Bloc and beyond, such as *Miasto Blok-How* (2012), *Blok Wschodni* (2014), *Blokowice* (2016), *Brutal London* (Prestel, 2016), *Brutal East* (2017), *The Constructivist* (2017), *Modern East* (2017), *Brutal Britain* (2018), *Hidden Cities* (2018), *Panelki* (2019), *Eastern Blocks* (2019), *Concrete Siberia* (2020), *Brutal Poland* (2020) and *Monotowns* (2021).

Brutal East vol. 2 is a follow-up to the worldwide-acclaimed *Brutal East* (Zupagrafika, 2017). The series enables readers to reconstruct some of the most interesting brutalist structures scattered around the former Eastern Bloc and ex-Yugoslavia, while learning about their architectural history.

Zupagrafika would like to thank Alexander Ostrogorsky, Maria Horowska, Kuba Snopek, Tetiana Kabakova, Alexander Veryovkin, Balázs Csizik, Les Johnstone, Giorgi Zatiashvili, Boris Jurmovski, Kseniya Lokotko, Peter Koppers, Alexey Kamensky, Oleg Belov, Maria Ważenicz, Maciej Kabsch, Marta & Maciej Mach, Paquita & Pepe, Kasia & Paweł, Andrés & Judit, Rita & Simón, for their help and support.

Copyright © 2021 ZUPAGRAFIKA

Design, illustrations, models, layout, cover, idea:
David Navarro & Martyna Sobecka (Zupagrafika)

Texts & edition:
David Navarro & Martyna Sobecka (Zupagrafika)

Foreword:
Alexander Ostrogorsky

CAD:
David Navarro & Maria Horowska (Zupagrafika)

Photographs:

David Navarro & Martyna Sobecka, Zupagrafika (Kyiv: pp. 4, 19, 34; Berlin: pp. 25, 26, 27)

Alexander Veryovkin (Moscow: pp. 9, 10, 11)

Balázs Csizik (Budapest: pp. 29, 30, 31)

Peter Koppers & Tetiana Kabakova (Kyiv: p. 17); Tetiana Kabakova (Kyiv: p. 18)

Giorgi Zatiashvili (Tbilisi: pp. 13, 14, 15)

Boris Jurmovski (Skopje: pp. 21, 22, 23)

Kseniya Lokotko (Minsk: pp. 33, 35)

Alexey Kamensky (Dombay: p. 37); Oleg Belov (Dombay: pp. 38-39)

Les Johnstone (Buzludzha: pp. 41, 42, 43)

All Rights Reserved. No part of this publication may be reproduced or transmitted in any form or by any means, electronic or mechanical, including photocopy, recording or any other information storage and retrieval system, without prior permission in writing from the publisher.

© for the cover, illustrations, models, text, design: Zupagrafika, 2021

© for the photos: Zupagrafika, with the exception of pp. 17, 37, 38-39, 41, 42, 43, back cover (their respective authors)

Published by Zupagrafika
Poznań, Poland. 2021

Printed in Poland
Paper from responsible sources
ISBN 978-83-950574-9-6
www.zupagrafika.com